Forensic Document Examination

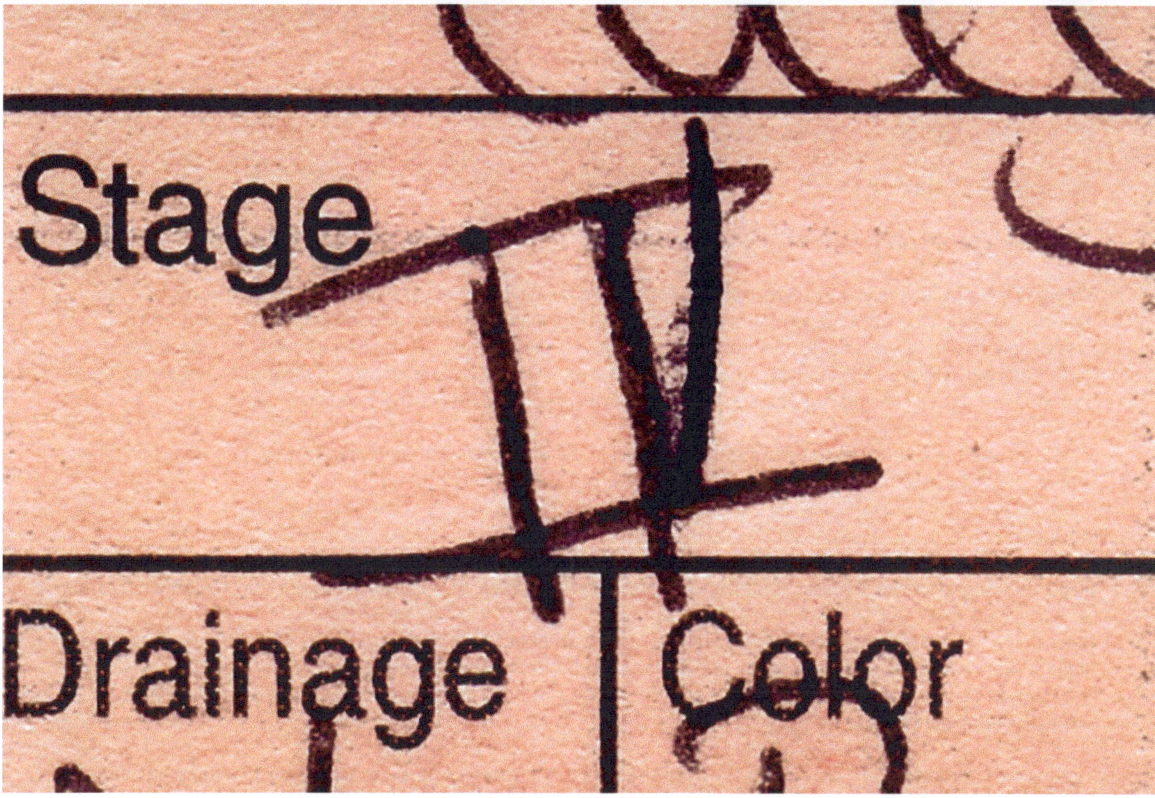

Forensic Document Examination

Fundamentals and Current Trends

Jane A. Lewis

ELSEVIER

AMSTERDAM • BOSTON • HEIDELBERG • LONDON • NEW YORK • OXFORD
PARIS • SAN DIEGO • SAN FRANCISCO • SINGAPORE • SYDNEY • TOKYO
Academic Press is an imprint of Elsevier

Academic Press is an imprint of Elsevier
The Boulevard, Langford Lane, Kidlington, Oxford, OX5 1GB
525 B Street, Suite 1800, San Diego, CA 92101-4495 USA

First published 2014

British Library Cataloguing in Publication Data
A catalogue record for this book is available from the British Library

Library of Congress Cataloging-in-Publication Data
A catalog record for this book is available from the Library of Congress

ISBN: 978-0-12-416693-6

For information on all Academic Press publications
visit our website at store.elsevier.com

Dedication

for Mickey Maier

Contents

Acknowledgments

I wish to thank Lisa Gordee for her help with photography and imaging. Anthony L. Chojnacki is due thanks for his vector drawings. Lloyd Cunningham deserves praise for his lovely calligraphy. Mickey Maier sustained me with his beer can chicken and planked salmon, for which I am thankful.

Introduction

The cover of this book shows a beautiful bank entrance. It fits with forensic document examination because many of the cases submitted to forensic document examiners include evidence types that originate in the banking system, such as forged checks, disputed signatures on loans, mortgages, personal guarantees, and bank robbery notes.

This book will enlighten forensic document examiners, attorneys, investigators, and others using the services of forensic document examiners with a bit of history, basic principles, and current trends in the science. Time has changed and improved the science of forensic document examination. We now apply standards that did not exist 20 years ago. Instrumentation has moved beyond the microscope and the magnifying glass to digital cameras, video spectral comparators, electrostatic detection devices for the development of indented writing on paper, scanners, and software programs to assist forensic document examiners.

Forensic document examiners are misunderstood by the general public and by attorneys who use our services. The public thinks that we perform personality assessments from handwriting. We do not. Attorneys are unable to separate the properly trained and qualified forensic document examiner from the graphologist or self-trained person on the fringes of the forensic science world. This book will help distinguish the properly trained forensic document examiner from those who lack the required education and initial professional training.

Attorneys, investigators, and forensic document examiners will appreciate the descriptions of state of the art practices, instruments, and research in forensic document examination. Standards and methodologies evolve and improve each year. This book captures the scientific progress of forensic document examination to date.

Topics featured include: the history of writing, the history of forensic document examination, the definition of forensic document examination, handwriting individuality, basic methodology, instrumentation, case examples, standards, court cases involving forensic document examination, court preparation, court charts, and research in the field.

eighth to mid-twelfth century
charlemagne
alcuin

carolingian minuscule

A Brief History of Writing

Chapter Outline

Forensic Document Examination. http://dx.doi.org/10.1016/B978-0-12-416693-6.00001-1

The past is never dead. It's not even past.
(William Faulkner, Requiem for a Nun, 1951)

Cave Paintings

In the beginning we communicated with pictures. Cave paintings dated between 20,000 and 35,000 BC show prehistoric man's early picture writing (Jackson, 1981). The walls of caves in Altamira, Spain and Lascaux, France bloom with painted images of bison, bulls, horses, and other animals (Fairbank, 1970). The intent of these early wall murals eludes scientists. But pictures on cave walls initiated the path to modern handwriting. Figure 1.1 shows an example of a horse painted on the wall of a Lascaux cave. Communication by pictures in ancient times grew into pictograms. Pictograms followed the bison and horses found on cave walls, but consisted of simpler designs (ibid.). Ideograms were word signs that represented ideas and actions as in road signs of today (ibid.). Eventually phonetic writing emerged. Each sign or phonogram represented language sounds, which ultimately lead to the alphabet (ibid.).

Cuneiform Writing

Cuneus comprises the Latin root of cuneiform, which means wedge. A triangular reed or stylus was used to form cuneiform signs in wet clay. Clay tablets were then dried in the sun to permanently fix the writing (Fairbank, 1970). Sumerian cuneiform existed as the first written language. The earliest examples date back

FIGURE 1.1 Vector drawing by Anthony Chojnacki of an image of a horse from Lascaux Caves. *http://en.wikipedia.org/wiki/File:Lascaux2.jpg (Accessed October 11, 2013), (http://commons.wikimedia.org/wiki/Commons:Copyright_tags#Various_free_licenses)*

to 3100 BC (ibid.). Sumerian civilization lived in the Fertile Crescent from 3500 to 1720 BC (Jackson, 1981). Figure 1.2 depicts a cuneiform tablet. During this same time period Chinese writing developed (Gaur, 1992).

Egyptian Writing

Ancient Egyptian writing consisted of three styles: hieroglyphic, hieratic, and demotic (Fairbank, 1970: 27). Figure 1.3 shows hieroglyphic picture-writing.

FIGURE 1.2 Vector drawing by Anthony Chojnacki of an image of a Sumerian inscription on a creamy stone plaque showing cuneiform script. *http://upload.wikimedia.org/wikipedia/commons/9/91/Sumerian_26th_c_Adab.jpg (Accessed October 11, 2013), (http://commons.wikimedia.org/wiki/Commons:Copyright_tags#Various_free_licenses)*

FIGURE 1.3 Vector drawing by Anthony Chojnacki of an image of cursive hieroglyphs from the Papyrus of Ani, an example of the Egyptian Book of the Dead. *http://en.wikipedia.org/wiki/Hieroglyphic (Accessed October 11, 2013), (http://commons.wikimedia.org/wiki/Commons:Copyright_tags#Various_free_licenses)*

Hieroglyphic writing appeared from 3100 BC to 400 AD. Hieratic and demotic evolved from the hieroglyphic script. Hieratic grew from the hieroglyphic writing, and was used from 3500 BC to 400 AD. The demotic, more cursive form of Egyptian writing was used from 600 BC to 500 AD (Gaur, 1992).

Phoenician Writing

Egyptian writing influenced the development of the Phoenician alphabet. Scientists speculate that the origin was in Greece, as early as 1000 BC (Fairbank, 1970). The coast of Syria provided a base for the Phoenicians. They survived as seafaring traders along the Mediterranean Sea (Jackson, 1981). Each symbol in the Phoenician alphabet represented one sound (ibid.). The Phoenician alphabet appears in Figure 1.4.

Greek Alphabet

The Greek alphabet evolved from the Phoenician alphabet beginning after 900 BC (Jackson, 1981). The Greeks added vowels to the consonant-only Phoenician alphabet. The first two letters of the Greek alphabet, alpha and beta, form the word alphabet (Fairbank, 1970). Figure 1.5 shows the Greek alphabet painted on a cup.

Etruscan Alphabet

The Etruscans predated the Romans in Italy. An abecedarium was found in Marsiliana d'Alberg, Italy,

FIGURE 1.4 Vector drawing by Anthony Chojnacki of an image of the Phoenician alphabet. *http://commons.wikimedia.org/wiki/File:Phoenician_Alphabet_ua.jpg (Accessed October 11, 2013), (http://commons.wikimedia.org/wiki/Commons:Copyright_tags#Various_free_licenses)*

in 700 BC (ibid.). The alphabet consisted of 26 letters. The arrangement on the page was laid down from right to left (ibid: 39). **Figure 1.6** shows an inscription on a warrior head used as an Etruscan grave marker.

Roman Alphabet

"Iacta alea est," (Latin: "The die has been cast") said Julius Caesar in 49 BC (Suetonius, 1913). He led his army across the Rubicon River in Northern Italy. The phrase means that something is inevitable or there is no turning back. During this time the Roman alphabet, which

FIGURE 1.5 Vector drawing by Anthony Chojnacki of an image of the early Greek alphabet painted on the body of an Attic black-figure cup at the National Archaeological Museum of Athens. *http://en.m.wikipedia.org/wiki/File:NAMA_Alphabet_grec.jpg (Accessed October 11, 2013), (creativecommons.org/licenses/by-sa/3.0/deed.en; http://commons.wikimedia.org/wiki/Commons:Copyright_tags#Various_free_licenses)*

evolved from the Greek alphabet, established preeminence as the script of the Roman Empire (Gaur, 1992). This alphabet included 26 letters and still exists in many cultures today. Figure 1.7 depicts an image of Roman lettering carved in marble.

FIGURE 1.6 Vector drawing by Anthony Chojnacki of an image of an Etruscan cippus (grave marker) in the form of a warrior head, found in the necropolis Crocifisso del Tufo outside Orvieto, Italy. This is a side view showing the inscription in the Old Italic alphabet. *https://commons.wikimedia.org/wiki/File:Etruscan_cippus_warrior_head_side.jpg (Accessed October 11, 2013), (http://commons.wikimedia.org/wiki/Commons:Copyright_tags#Various_free_licenses)*

Word Separation in Manuscripts

Before the seventh century, Latin manuscripts contained connected words with no spaces, *scriptura continua*, rather than separated words. The development of silent reading led to the need for separation of words. The first Latin manuscript with separated words was the Irish *Book of Mulling* (before 692 AD) (Saenger, 1997).

FIGURE 1.7 Vector drawing by Anthony Chojnacki of a marble sign in Roman lettering in the Collegio degli Augustali in Herculaneum in Italy. *http://en.m.wikipedia.org/wiki/File:Herculaneum_Collegio_degli_Augustali_Iscrizione.jpg (Accessed October 11, 2013), (http://commons.wikimedia.org/wiki/Commons:Copyright_tags#Various_free_licenses)*

Carolingian Minuscule

The emperor Charlemagne (742–814 AD) unified Western Europe and promoted the Carolingian miniscule style of writing (Gaur, 1992). Clarity and decorative capital letters characterized the script (ibid.). The rounded Carolingian miniscule writing appears in **Figure 1.8**.

Gothic Script

Gothic style script advanced in the 12th and 13th centuries (ibid.). Angular, heavy, and vertical writing

FIGURE 1.8 Handwriting sample of Carolingian Miniscule.

represented the style. Figure 1.9 shows an example of Gothic style script. Gothic style lasted until the 16th century AD (ibid.). The *New York Times* title is written in a textured gothic script called Gothic Textura Quadrata (Florey, 2009). This style appears in Figure 1.10.

Italic Script

Niccolo Niccoli (1364–1437), a Florentine scholar, is credited with inventing italic writing (Fairbank, 1970). Italic writing in the 1500s progressed very close to a cursive style (Gaur, 1992). Notice the more simplified "a" in the writing by Niccoli in Figure 1.11. The word italic reflects the Italian origin of the style (Florey, 2009).

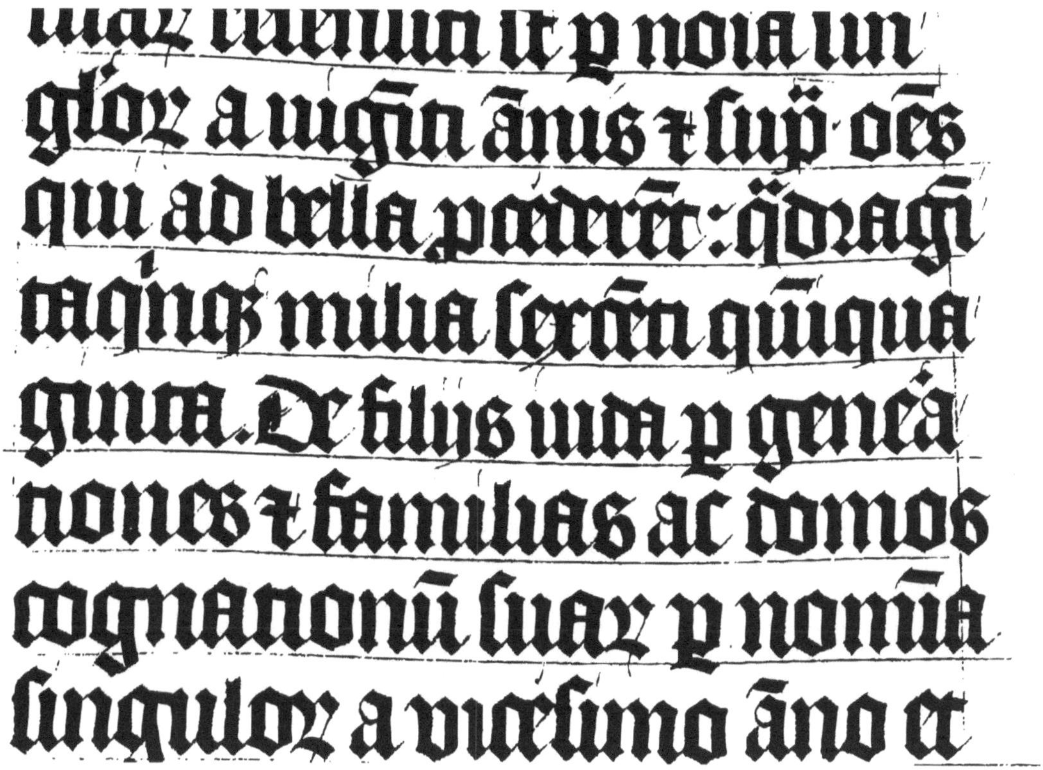

FIGURE 1.9 Vector drawing by Anthony Chojnacki of gothic calligraphy in a Latin Bible of AD 1407 on display in Malmesbury Abbey, Wiltshire, England. The Bible was handwritten in Belgium by Gerard Brils, for reading aloud in a monastery. Taken by Adrian Pingstone in February 2005 and released to the public domain. *http://commons.wikimedia.org/wiki/File:Calligraphy.malmesbury.bible.arp.jpg (Accessed October 11, 2013), (http://commons.wikimedia.org/wiki/Commons:Copyright_tags#Various_free_licenses)*

FIGURE 1.10 Handwriting sample of Gothic Textura Quadrata.

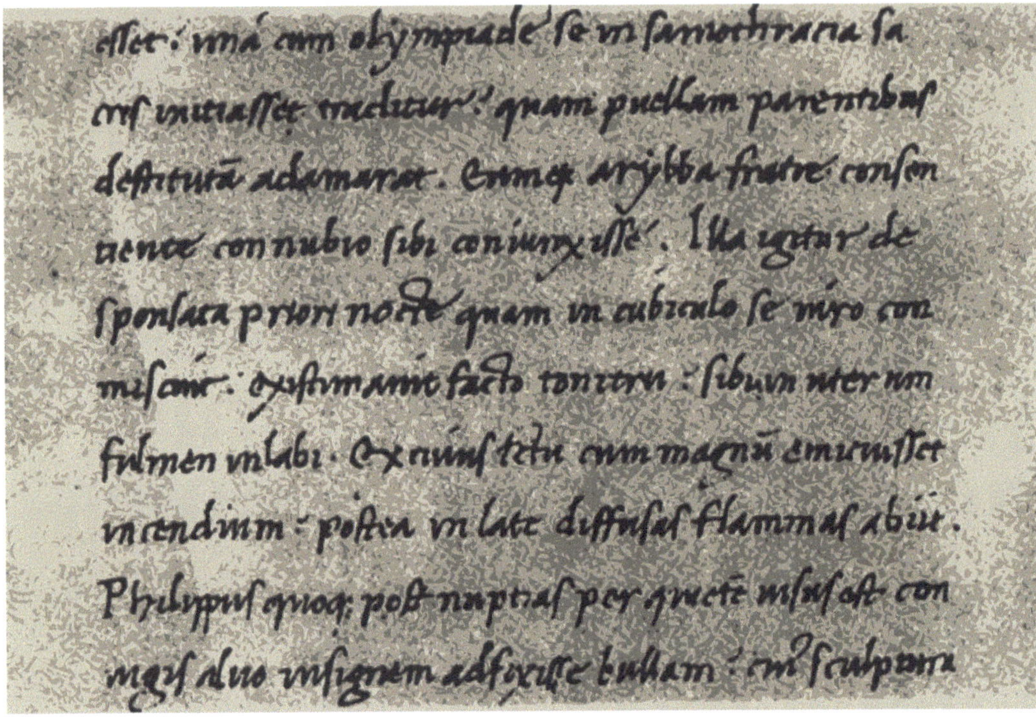

FIGURE 1.11 Vector drawing by Anthony Chojnacki of handwriting by Niccolo de Niccoli (1364–1437), which served as the origin of italic type. *https://en.wikipedia.org/wiki/File:Niccolo_de_Niccoli_italic_handwriting.jpg (Accessed October 11, 2013), (http://commons.wikimedia.org/wiki/Commons:Copyright_tags#Various_free_licenses)*

Copperplate Handwriting

Copperplate calligraphy acquired the name from the copperplates used to engrave images of handwriting for copybooks in the 1600s (Henning, 2002). People originally referred to Copperplate as Roundhand. Elegance and legibility described the writing (ibid.). Copperplate handwriting occurred commonly in the 18th and early 19th centuries. Figure 1.12 exemplifies Copperplate style writing. Spencerian writing advanced from Copperplate writing (ibid.).

FIGURE 1.12 Handwriting sample of Copperplate script.

FIGURE 1.13 Calligraphy of an address on an envelope.

Calligraphy

Calligraphy comes from the Greek word kalligraphia, which means "beautiful writing." Today calligraphy refers to generally aesthetically pleasing writing (ibid.). Specialized pointed and broad-tipped pens and brushes are used to write in calligraphy. The term "penmanship" used to mean calligraphy in the United States before 1950. Calligraphy from a colleague of mine appears in **Figure 1.13**.

Modern Handwriting

The Palmer Method

Austin Norman Palmer (1860–1927) attended the Bryant & Stratton Business School in Manchester, New Hampshire, where he became a fine penman (ibid.). He eventually opened his own school and had a penmanship publication. He developed the Palmer Method. It

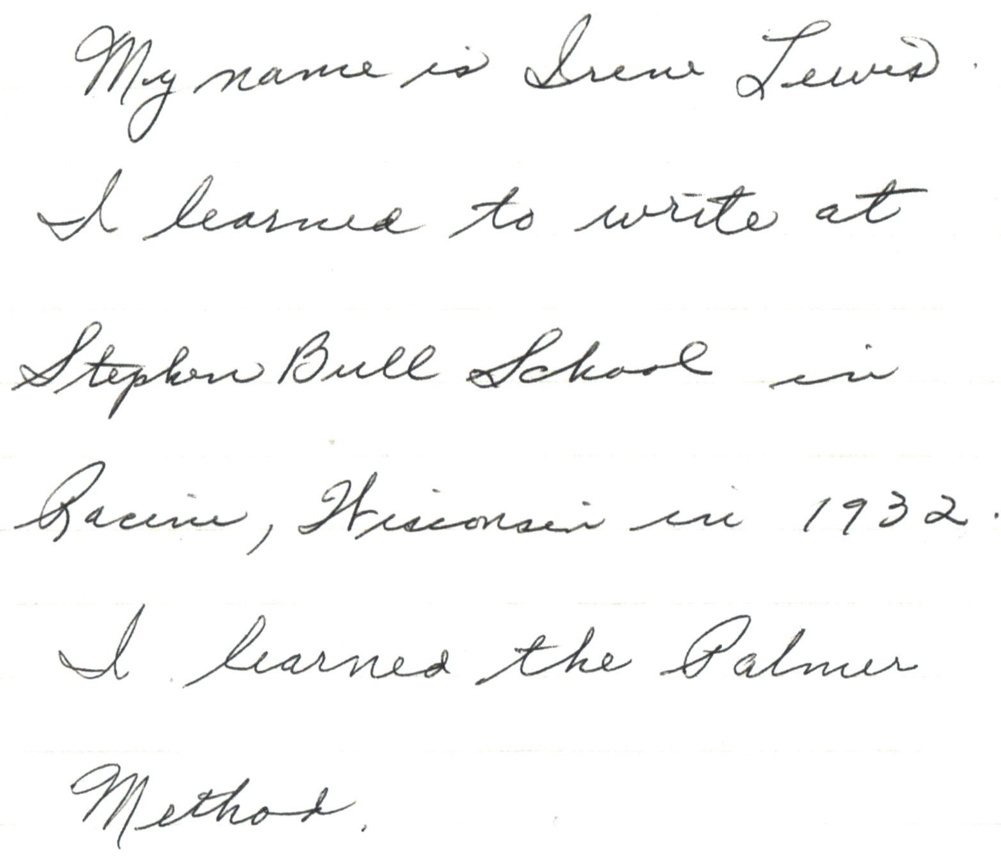

FIGURE 1.14 The Palmer Method of handwriting written by Irene Lewis in 2013.

emphasized writing with clarity, speed, and few flourishes. His method spread throughout the United States, particularly in Catholic grade schools. Students began by making ovals and up and down strokes (called push pulls). He promoted a light touch and forearm motion (ibid.). The Palmer Method is still in use in the United States today. Figure 1.14 shows a Palmer Method cursive writing sample from my mother.

Zaner–Bloser

Charles P. Zaner (1864–1918) published his modern business writing system in the 1890s in the United States

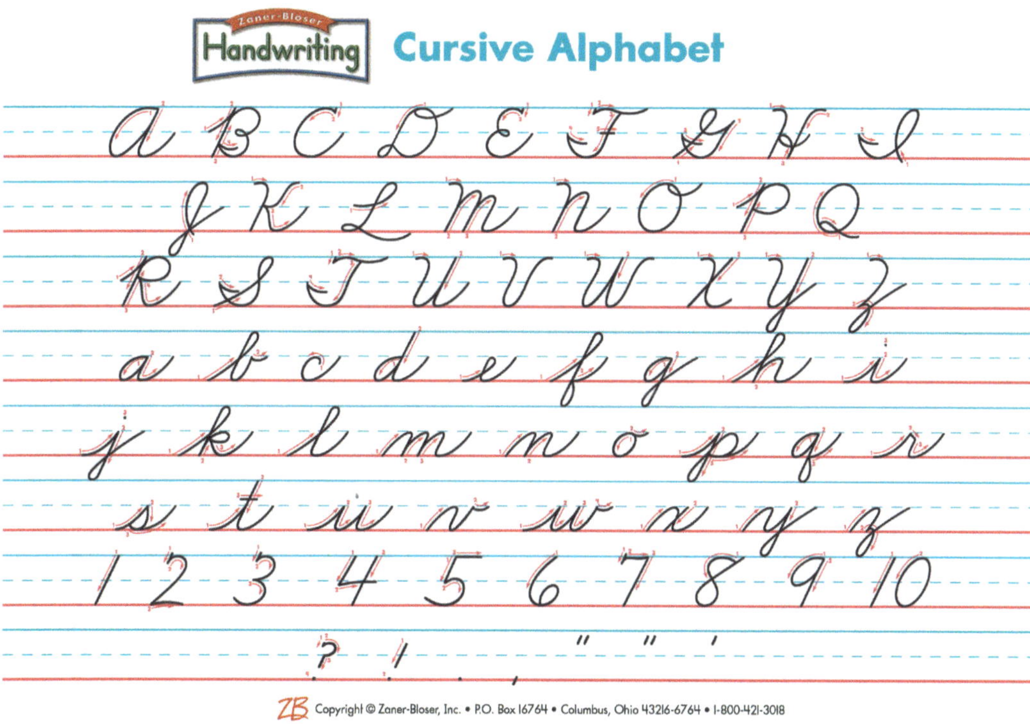

FIGURE 1.15 Zaner–Bloser cursive alphabet. *(Used by permission)*

FIGURE 1.16 Zaner–Bloser hand printed alphabet. *(Used by permission)*

(ibid.). He founded the Zanarian College of Penmanship in Columbus, Ohio, in 1888 (ibid.).

Elmer Ward Bloser established a partnership with Charles Zaner. Bloser became a penmanship master (ibid.). The Zaner–Bloser handwriting system shares similarities in style with modern systems like the Palmer Method. Schools in the United States still use the Zaner–Bloser system today. Cursive and hand printed samples of the Zaner–Bloser handwriting system are shown in **Figure 1.15** and **Figure 1.16**.

FIGURE 1.17 Vector drawing by Anthony Chojnacki of a modern pictogram of an airplane. *https://commons.wikimedia.org/wiki/File:National_Park_Service_sample_pictographs.svg (Accessed October 11, 2013), (http://commons.wikimedia.org/wiki/Commons:Copyright_tags#Various_free_licenses)*

Modern Pictograms

We have traveled through time beginning with pictures on Stone Age cave walls and ending with the modern pictogram of an airplane depicted in **Figure 1.17**.

References

Fairbank, A., 1970. The Story of Handwriting. Watson-Guptill Publications, New York.

Florey, K., 2009. Script & Scribble: The Rise and Fall of Handwriting. Melville House Publishing, Brooklyn, New York.

Gaur, A., 1992. A History of Writing. Cross River Press, New York, London, Paris.

Henning, W., 2002. An Elegant Hand. Oak Knoll Press, New Castle, Delaware.

Jackson, D., 1981. The Story of Writing. Taplinger Publishing Co., Inc., New York.

Saenger, P., 1997. Space Between Words: The Origins of Silent Reading. Stanford University Press, Stanford, California.

Suetonius, C. Tranquillus, 1913. The Lives of the Twelve Caesars, Loeb Classical Library, The Life of Julius Caesar, paragraph 32.

CHAPTER 2

The History of Forensic Document Examination

Chapter Outline

Forensic Document Examination. http://dx.doi.org/10.1016/B978-0-12-416693-6.00002-3

History is written by the winners.
(Alex Haley, interview with David Frost, April 20, 1972)

Daniel T. Ames

In the 1800s penmanship teachers and master penmen taught Americans to write beautifully. They penned lovely calling cards used by ladies and gentlemen. Skillful writing was prized. Penmen of the late 1800s and early 1900s founded penmanship magazines, writing schools, and books on various handwriting methods.

In 1901, Theodore Roosevelt was President of the United States, women did not yet have the right to vote (Library of Congress, 2013), and Daniel T. Ames, founder of the *Penman's Art Journal of New York* and author of *Ames' Compendium of Practical and Artistic Penmanship*, published one of the early texts on forensic document examination, *Ames on Forgery* (Ames, 1901).

Daniel Ames completed 30 years as an Examiner of Contested Handwriting in 1901 (ibid.). His book described correctly the individuality of handwriting. More than 50 cases of disputed handwriting, including illustrations of charts and evidence, appear in the book. His work was used in several "cause celebre" cases like the Molineux poisoning murder trial and the Dreyfus case from France (ibid.).

Ames got it right on the individuality of each person's handwriting, which research like Sargur Srihari's paper, *The Individuality of Handwriting*, confirmed (Srihari, 2002). Ames' belief in the accuracy of graphology (the art of determining character from handwriting) proved wrong. In Chapter 1 in *Ames on Forgery* (ibid.), "Personality in Handwriting," he displays the signatures of United States historical figures John Hancock and John Adams, two signers of the Declaration of Independence. He then states, "the bold, strong character of these men stands out in their autographs" (ibid.). This opinion, that personality can be detected from examination of handwriting, was not based on any scientific testing or research. Ames relied instead on his strong belief and intuition about graphology. Research reveals that graphology is unreliable and performs no better than chance (Klimoski et al., 1983; Ben-Shakhar et al., 1986).

Ames also said that he could determine the sex of a writer from examination of a handwriting sample (Ames, 1901). Forensic document examiners today know that this is not true. In my early training at the FBI Laboratory, US Secret Service Laboratory, and the Wisconsin State Crime Laboratory in Milwaukee, fundamental principles of forensic document examination included:

1. Handwriting is individual.

2. Each person has natural variation in his or her handwriting.

3. Each person has a skill level that he or she generally cannot surpass.

4. It is not possible to determine age or sex from handwriting.

The progressive ferment of the turn of the century in 1901 left Daniel Ames untouched. He relied on tired stereotypes regarding writing of the different sexes. He said "the greater and more heroic things of life engage the attention of men, while women are led by their nature and instinct into the more circumscribed realm of social and domestic life" (ibid.). I wonder how many conversations Ames had with suffragettes in 1901.

Penmanship teachers like Ames became the early forensic document examiners. Their work with thousands of writings was the foundation for understanding how to distinguish the handwritings of different writers. They were the early expert witnesses called to testify in cases of forged checks, threatening letters, disputed wills, and general signature disputes.

Albert S. Osborn

Albert S. Osborn (Figure 2.1) claims the title the "Father of Questioned Documents." At a recent scientific conference, forensic document examiner colleagues sported buttons that read, "I'm An Osbornian." Albert Osborn applied scientific principles to questioned document problems. This is in contrast to poorly

FIGURE 2.1 Albert S. Osborn. (*Used by permission of John Paul Osborn*)

trained practitioners then and now who are often self-trained and work by applying intuition to cases of questioned documents.

Albert S. Osborn (1858–1946) was born in the state of Michigan. He attended the State College at Lansing, and in 1882 began a position as a penmanship teacher at Rochester Business Institute (ASQDE, 2013). Teaching handwriting evolved into an interest in the identification of handwriting, typewriting, paper, ink, and other questioned document problems (ibid.). Mr. Osborn transitioned to full time work as a forensic document examiner in 1920 in New York City (ibid.). He met informally for many years with colleagues at his home to discuss research and methodology in the examination of questioned documents. In 1942, the group formed a formal association. The American Society of Questioned Document Examiners was formed with Albert S. Osborn as the first president (ibid.).

The increased use of business documents in the 20th century created work for forensic document examiners (FDEs). Albert Osborn's application of science to questioned document problems provided ample material for his extensive textbook, *Questioned Documents* (Osborn, 1910). He wrote a second edition of *Questioned Documents* in 1929 (Osborn, 1929). Topics in the second edition include: preliminary examinations, classification of questioned documents, standards for comparison, photography of questioned documents, the microscope and questioned documents, movement in writing, variation in genuine writing, the comparison process, simulated forgeries, anonymous letters, graphology, ink, order of writing, erasures, age of document, typewriting, questioned document cases in court, and the law and legal procedure in disputed document cases (Osborn, 1929).

Unlike Daniel Ames, Albert Osborn treated graphology with disdain. He studied and investigated the claims that graphology could indeed determine personality from the examination of a sample of handwriting. Osborn concluded that, "the definite conclusion is reached that this method of investigation, at least in its present state of development, is of little if any value as an aid in the discovery and proof of the facts in any kind of questioned document inquiry" (Osborn, 1929).

In 1932, Albert Osborn testified in the Lindberg baby kidnapping case (*New Jersey v. Bruno Hauptman*) along with seven other FDEs, who all identified Hauptman as the writer (ABFDE website, 2013).

Other Pioneers of Forensic Document Examination

Ordway Hilton (1913–1998) wrote one of the primary FDE texts, *Scientific Examination of Questioned Documents*, in 1956, and a revised edition in 1982 (Hilton, 1982). Mr. Hilton continued Albert S. Osborn's scientific approach to questioned document problems.

Wilson R. Harrison was an FDE and Director of the Forensic Science Laboratory in Llanishen, Cardiff, Wales. His text, *Suspect Documents*, was published in 1958 (Harrison, 1958). His book continued the able application of science to questioned document cases.

In 1959, another fine early FDE text was written by James V.P. Conway, *Evidential Documents* (Conway, 1959). Mr. Conway was an Examiner of Questioned Documents and Postal Inspector in charge of the San Francisco Identification Laboratory of the U.S. Postal Inspection Service.

Donald Doud (1916–2005) was an eminent FDE who worked from Milwaukee, Wisconsin. Cases of note during Mr. Doud's long career are described in the book, *Witness to Forgery* (Doud, 2009).

David Ellen is the former Head of the Questioned Documents Section of the Metropolitan Police Forensic Science Laboratory in London, England. His book, *The Scientific Examination of Documents: Methods and Techniques* (Ellen, 1989), explained modern instrumentation and examination methods used by FDEs. The third edition of his book was published in 2006 (Ellen, 2006).

Questioned Document Organizations

American Society of Questioned Document Examiners (ASQDE) was founded in 1942 (ASQDE website, 2013).

The American Academy of Forensic Sciences (AAFS) was founded in 1948 (AAFS website, 2013). James Clark Sellers was elected the first Questioned Document Section Chair of AAFS in 1950 (Riordan et al., 2013). The American Board of Forensic Document Examiners (ABFDE) began in 1977 (ABFDE website, 2013).

ASTM Committee E30 on Forensic Science was formed in 1970 (ASTM website, 2013).

TWGDOC formed in 1997, and later changed to SWGDOC (Scientific Working Group for Forensic Document Examination.) (SWGDOC website, 2013).

Forensic Laboratories Established with Questioned Document Sections

The Scientific Crime Detection Laboratory in Chicago, Illinois, was an early forensic science laboratory in the United States. It was established in 1938 (Riordan et al., 2013).

The Alcohol, Tobacco and Firearms Laboratory originated from an act of Congress in 1886 (McClary, 2013).

In 1914, the Canadian LSJML Laboratory in Montreal, Quebec was founded. By 1970, a questioned document section had joined the organization (Campbell, 2013).

The Federal Bureau of Investigation (FBI) Laboratory in Washington, D.C. was established in 1932 (FBI website, 2013).

The Royal Canadian Mounted Police Laboratory (RCMP) began in 1938 in Regina, Saskatchewan, Canada, followed by the Ottawa Laboratory, which opened in 1942 (Campbell, 2013).

The Department of Veterans Affairs Laboratory in Washington, D.C. originated in 1939 (Singer, 2013).

The United States Postal Inspection Services Forensic Laboratory now located in Dulles, Virginia started work in 1946 (Beal, 2013).

The United States Secret Service Forensic Services Division formed in 1974 (Storer, 2013).

Immigration & Customs Enforcement Laboratory in McLean, Virginia, began in 1978 (ICE website, 2013).

The Internal Revenue Service National Forensic Laboratory in Chicago originated in 1973 after a separation from the Bureau of Alcohol, Tobacco and Firearms (Fitzgerald, 1995).

Revenue Canada opened in 1995. This laboratory evolved into Canada Border Services Agency (Campbell, 2005).

The United States Army Criminal Investigations Laboratory started in 1943 (Army CID website, 2013).

References

AAFS, American Academy of Forensic Sciences website: http://www.aafs.org/about-aafs (accessed 11.10.13).

ABFDE, American Board of Forensic Document Examiners website: http://www.abfde.org/ (accessed 11.10.13).

Ames, D., 1901. Ames on Forgery. The Boston Book Company, Boston.

Army, US Army Criminal Investigation Command website: http://www.cid.army.mil/ (accessed 11.10.13).

ASQDE, American Society of Questioned Document Examiners website: http://www.asqde.org/ (accessed 11.10.13).

ASTM, American Society for Testing and Materials International website: http://www.astm.org/ (accessed 11.10.13).

Beal, B., personal communication. 2013.

Ben-Shakhar, G., Bar-Hillel, M., Bilu, Y., Ben-Abba, E., Flug, A., 1986. Can Graphology Predict Occupational Success? Two Empirical Studies and Some

Methodological Ruminations. J. Appl. Psychol. 7 (4), 645–653.

Campbell, T., personal communication. 2013.

Conway, J., 1959. Evidential Documents. Charles C. Thomas, Springfield, Illinois.

Doud, D., 2009. Witness to Forgery. Orchard Knoll Publishers, Elm Grove, Wisconsin.

Ellen, D., 1989. The Scientific Examination of Documents: Methods and Techniques. Ellis Horwood Limited Chichester, West Sussex, England.

Ellen, D., 2006. Scientific Examination of Documents: Methods and Techniques, Third ed. CRC Press, Taylor & Francis Group, Boca Raton, Florida.

FBI, Federal Bureau of Investigation website: http://www.fbi.gov/about-us/lab (accessed 11.10.13).

Fitzgerald, M., 1995. History of the IRS National Forensic Lab (unpublished).

Harrison, W., 1958. Suspect Documents: Their Scientific Examination. Praeger, New York.

Hilton, O., 1982. Scientific Examination of Questioned Documents, Revised Edition. Elsevier North Holland, Inc., New York.

ICE Homeland Securities Investigations Forensic Laboratory website: http://www.ice.gov/hsi-fl/ (accessed 11.10.13).

Klimoski, R.J., Rafaeli, A., 1983. Inferring Personal Qualities Through Handwriting Analysis. J. Occupational Psychol. 56, 191–202.

Library of Congress website: http://www.loc.gov/index.html (accessed 10.24.13).

McClary, C., personal communication. 2013.

Osborn, A., 1929. Questioned Documents, Second ed. Nelson-Hall, Chicago.

Riordan, W., Gustafson, J., Fitzgerald, M., Lewis, J., 2013. Forensic Document Examination. In: Ubelaker, D. (Eds.), Forensic Science Current Issues. Future Directions, Wiley-Blackwell, Chichester, West Sussex, UK, pp. 224–251.

Singer, K., personal communication. 2013.

Srihari, S., 2002. The Individuality of Handwriting. J. Forensic Sci. 47 (4), 856–872.

Storer, K., personal communication. 2013.

SWGDOC, Scientific Working Group for Forensic Document Examination website: http://www.swgdoc.org/ (accessed 11.10.13).

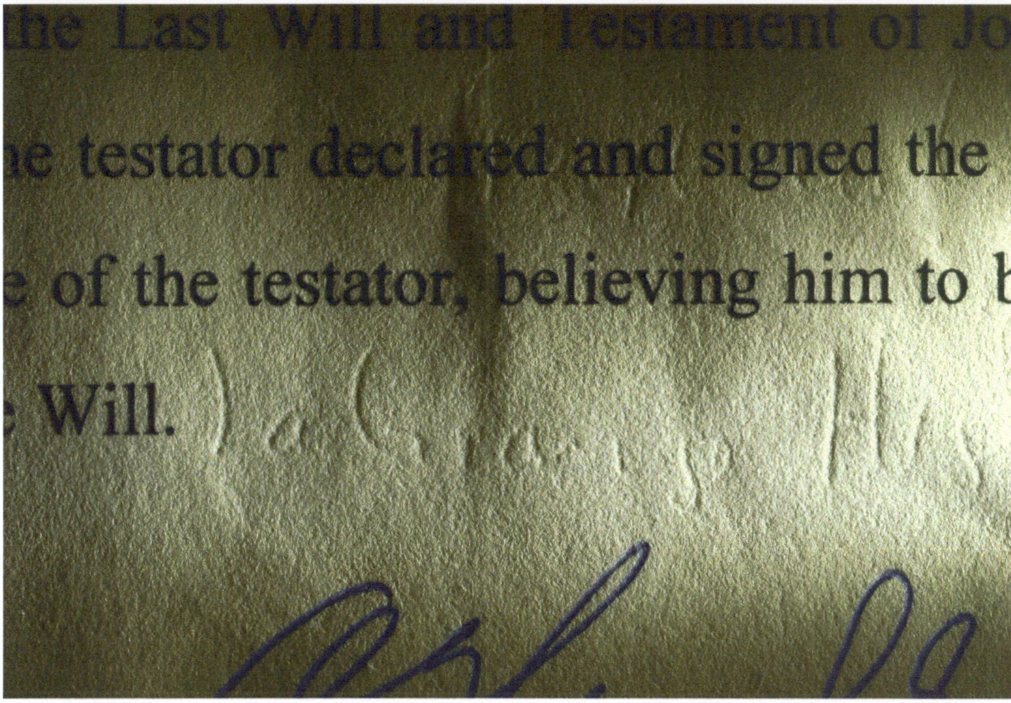

CHAPTER 3

Forensic Document Examination Defined

Chapter Outline

Forensic Document Examination. http://dx.doi.org/10.1016/B978-0-12-416693-6.00003-5

Equipped with his five senses, man explores the universe around him and calls the adventure Science.
(Edwin Powell Hubble, The Nature of Science, 1954)

Forensic Document Examination

"The profession of an FDE or examiner of questioned documents grew out of the courts' need for assistance in interpreting evidence relating to the preparation and subsequent treatment of documents. It is actually a pure forensic science in that it developed within the legal system rather than as an extension of other professions, such as medicine, dentistry, chemistry, or engineering."
(Lindblom, 2006: 10)

Forensic science is the application of science to the law. Forensic document examination, latent print examination, DNA, forensic imaging, pathology, drug chemistry, and physical chemistry all fit this description. Forensic document examination is often overlooked and misunderstood by the public. P.D. James understood the basic work of forensic document examiners. In her 1977 book *Death of an Expert Witness* (James, 1977), a forensic document examiner was a central character and suspect in the murder of a forensic scientist in a laboratory in England. A forensic document examiner made a minor appearance in the German movie *The Lives of Others* (*Das Leben der*

Anderen; Henckel von Donnersmarck, 2006). The movie is about the effect of Stasi agents spying on East Berlin citizens shortly before the fall of the Berlin Wall in 1989. A forensic document examiner demonstrated a chart that identified a particular typewriter by comparing the questioned with known typewriting. All typewriters at the time were registered in East Berlin.

Forensic document examination is the application of science and analytical techniques to questions concerning documents. David Ellen, in his book *Scientific Examination of Documents* (Ellen, 2006: 1), said, "Scientific method is a way of thinking." He applied the scientific method to the examination of documents by observing "...the testing of various parameters and reference to the background knowledge on the subject in order to reach a conclusion" (ibid.).

ASTM Standard E444-09, *Standard Guide for Scope of the Work of Forensic Document Examiners,* describes the work of FDEs thus: "The forensic document examiner makes scientific examinations, comparisons, and analyses of documents in order to: (1) establish genuineness or nongenuineness, or to expose forgery, or to reveal alterations, additions, or deletions, (2) identify or eliminate persons as the source of handwriting, (3) identify or eliminate the source of typewriting or other impression, marks, or relative evidence, and (4) write reports or give testimony, when needed, to aid the users of the examiner's services in understanding the examiner's findings." (ASTM E444-09, 2013).

Forensic document examiner (FDE), Questioned Document Examiner, Document Analyst, Document Examiner, and Handwriting Expert are all titles applied to practitioners. Handwriting Expert is not completely accurate because the work involves more diverse examinations than simply handwriting. Most practitioners today refer to themselves as forensic document examiners (FDE). We work in local, state, and federal laboratories, and also in private practice. Typical cases submitted to FDEs include: forged checks, threatening letters, disputed signatures on wills, trusts, business documents, mortgage documents, typewritten documents, altered business documents, medical records, and photocopied documents.

FDEs most often compare questioned writing with known writings for identification or elimination purposes. Forensic handwriting identification is based on the principle that no two people write exactly alike.

In a recent case, a disputed signature on a will was submitted to me for examination. A comparison was made with more than 20 contemporaneous known signatures of the deceased person. The background knowledge on the subject included detailed description in the forensic document literature of the characteristics of simulated signatures. Adding to the background knowledge on the subject was my education and specialized training in forensic document examination. A detailed examination of the questioned signature visually and microscopically, and comparison of the questioned signature with the contemporaneous known samples, backed up the hypothesis that the signature was a simulated forgery.

Graphology

Getting back to the confusion surrounding forensic document examination mentioned above, the general public thinks that forensic document examiners determine personality from handwriting. Forensic document examination is not graphology. Graphology is the art of determining personality from handwriting. Graphology may be learned by taking a correspondence course or reading a pamphlet on the subject. Graphologists have sold their services to companies for use as a hiring tool. Companies in France routinely require a handwriting sample submission as part of a job application. Years ago, a Milwaukee business used a graphologist instead of a psychologist to screen applications because the graphologist was cheaper than the psychologist and provided the same service.

Many people wish to believe in graphology, but the research fails to validate it. An article published in the *Journal of Applied Psychology* in 1986 found through studies that graphologists used for personnel selection performed no better than chance (Ben-Shakhar et al., 1986). Graphology was again tested by finding 17 studies examining the validity of the practice and comparing the accuracy of graphologists in using handwriting to predict successful job performance (Neter et al., 1989). Psychologists performed better than graphologists in the study (ibid.). Klimoski and

Rafaeli also considered graphology as an employment assessment tool and did not find it useful (Klimoski et al., 1989). A British study (Furnam et al., 2003) found that graphology did not reliably predict personality.

Graphologists would be of little interest to FDEs if they limited themselves to a booth at the state fair; unfortunately many of these practitioners present themselves in civil and criminal trials as forensic document examiners. Judges have allowed these graphologists, self-trained as FDEs, to testify in court. Not every judge allows unqualified graphologists to testify. According to Paul Giannelli writing in *Criminal Justice Magazine* from the American Bar Association's Criminal Justice Section: "In *United States v. Bourgeois*, 950 F. 2nd 980 (5th Cir. 1992), the Fifth Circuit upheld a trial court's exclusion of the testimony of an 'expert' who was not a member of the American Board of Forensic Document Examiners, who practiced graphotherapy in addition to handwriting comparison, and who acquired a master's degree in graphoanalysis and a Ph.D. in metaphysics and religion by correspondence" (Giannelli, 2004).

Training of Forensic Document Examiners

The only way to acquire training as an FDE is through a fulltime, two-year apprenticeship in a recognized forensic laboratory in the public sector or in a recognized private laboratory. It is not possible to become an FDE through self-study or a correspondence class.

The principal trainer must have acquired his or her training in a recognized forensic laboratory.

Certification

The American Board of Forensic Document Examiners (ABFDE) was formed in 1977. The certification program identifies qualified FDEs who work in government laboratories and private laboratories in the United States, Canada, Australia, and New Zealand. The ABFDE is incorporated in the District of Columbia. Sponsors of the ABFDE include: the American Society of Questioned Document Examiners, the Canadian Society of Forensic Science, the Southeastern Association of Forensic Document Examiners, and the Southwestern Association of Forensic Document Examiners. The ABFDE is recognized by the American Academy of Forensic Sciences, the International Association of Identification, the Mid-Atlantic Association of Forensic Scientists, and the Midwestern Association of Forensic Scientists.

The ABFDE Requirements for Certification are as follows (ABFDE, 2013):

1. Applicants must possess good moral character, integrity, and high ethics.

2. Applicants must be permanent residents of the United States of America, Canada, Australia, or New Zealand.

3. Applicants must have earned at least a baccalaureate degree from an accredited academic institution.

4. Applicants must complete a two-year, full-time training program in a forensic laboratory recognized by the ABFDE.

5. Applicants must have three ABFDE-certified FDEs as references.

6. Applicants must be actively working as an FDE.

7. Applicants must successfully complete a written, practical, and oral examination based on typical cases encountered by FDEs.

8. A candidate will be recognized as a Diplomate of the ABFDE upon successful completion of the testing program.

References

ABFDE, American Board of Forensic Document Examiners: http://www.abfde.org (accessed 11.10.13).

ASTM E444-09, Standard Guide for Scope of the Work of Forensic Document Examiners: http://www.astm.org/Standards/E444.htm (accessed 11.10.13).

Ben-Shakhar, G., Bar-Hillel, M., Bilu, Y., Ben-Abba, E., Flug, A., 1986. Can Graphology Predict Occupational Success? Two Empirical Studies and Some Methodological Ruminations. J. Appl. Psychol. 71 (4), 645–653.

Ellen, D., 2006. Scientific Examination of Documents, Third ed. CRC Press, Taylor & Francis Group, Boca Raton, Florida, p.1.

Furnam, A., Chamorro-Premuzic, T., Callahan, I., 2003. Does Graphology Predict Personality and Intelligence? Individual Differences Res. J. 1 (2), 78–94.

Giannelli, P., Spring 2004. Expert Qualifications: Who Are These Guys? Criminal Justice Magazine 19 (1): http://www.americanbar.org/publications/criminal_justice_magazine_home/crimjust_cjmag_19_1_scientific.html (accessed 11.10.13).

Henckel von Donnersmarck, F., 2006. The Lives of Others, Sony Pictures Classics.

James, P.D., 1977. Death of an Expert Witness. Faber & Faber, London, UK.

Klimoski, R.J., Rafaeli, A., 1989. Inferring Personal Qualities through Handwriting Analysis. J. Occupational Psychol. 56, 191–202.

Lindblom, B., 2006. What Is Forensic Document Examination? In: Kelly, J.S., Lindblom, B. (Eds.), Scientific Examination of Questioned Documents, Second ed. CRC Press, Taylor & Francis Group, Boca Raton, Florida, p. 10.

Neter, E., Ben-Shakhar, G., 1989. The Predictive Validity of Graphological Inferences: A Meta-Analytic Approach. Personality and Individual Differences 10 (7), 737–745.

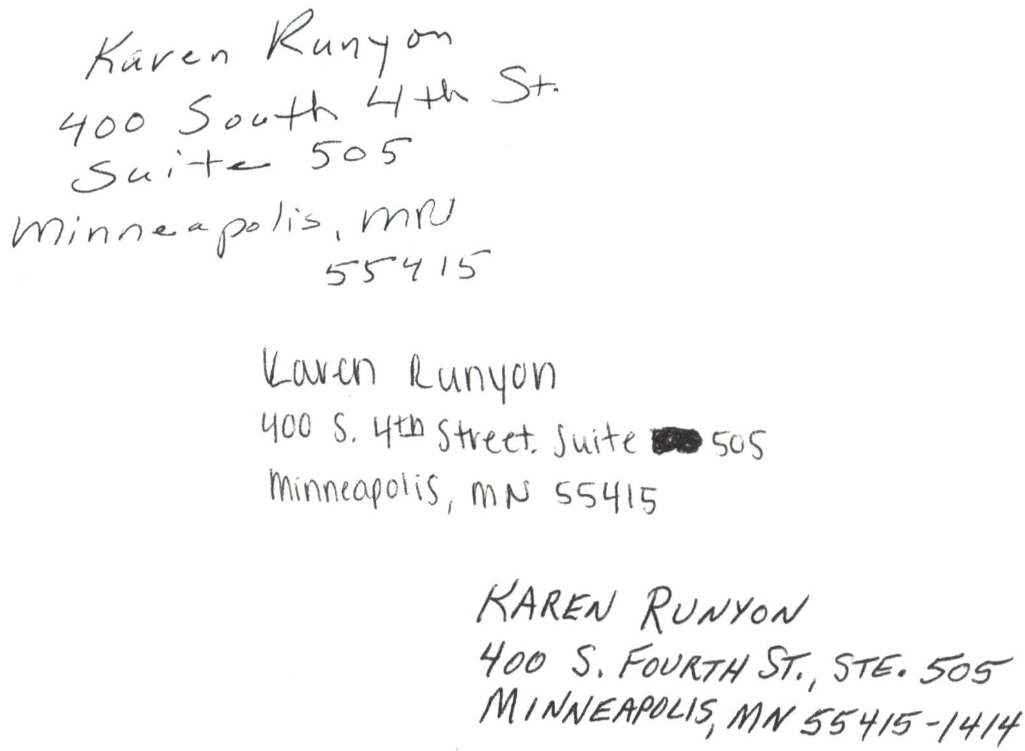

Handwriting Individuality

Chapter Outline

Forensic Document Examination. http://dx.doi.org/10.1016/B978-0-12-416693-6.00004-7

[I]f a man is not faithful to his own individuality he cannot be loyal to anything.
(Claude McKay, A Long Way from Home, 1937)

Individuality in Handwriting

No two people write exactly alike. Individual characteristics develop in each person's handwriting and they repeat themselves. These handwriting characteristics are used by the trained FDE to determine whether a person did or did not write a questioned document. The individuality of handwriting remains an accepted basic principle in forensic document examination. Albert Osborn in his book *Questioned Documents* (Osborn, 1929) said, "Handwriting is individualized from the very beginning of learning to write, but this development becomes much more pronounced as soon as writing is used to any considerable extent for practical purposes and its distinct individuality develops much earlier with some writers than others." Ordway Hilton went on to explain: "With the innumerable problems which have been submitted to document examiners throughout the years, there has never been found an example of two writers with identical handwriting" (Hilton, 1963).

Handwriting individuality is well accepted and relied upon by society in general, as evidenced by the use of signatures on identification and business documents such as driver licenses, wills, trusts, beneficiary forms, mortgage documents, certified mail receipts, marriage licenses, divorce documents, tax forms, loan documents, bank signature cards, delivery receipts, and digitized signature pads in stores.

Research

A robust body of research by FDEs and academic researchers supports the principle of uniqueness of an individual's handwriting, including:

1. A State University of New York study titled *Individuality of Handwriting* (Srihari, 2002) found that each of the 1,500 writers involved could be identified with a computer system using only a few handwriting characteristics with a 98% confidence level. FDEs consider more than a few handwriting characteristics in an examination of handwriting. The author speculated that the confidence level would reach 100% using more handwriting characteristics than the limited number used in the study.

2. A study titled *The Determination of Authorship from a Homogenous Group of Writers* used a group of writers from the same parochial grade school in New York. They all learned the Palmer Method of handwriting in their school. FDEs examined the handwriting of the New York school writers. The goal was to determine whether writers from a homogeneous group (they all learned the same handwriting style in the same school) could have their handwriting identified by FDEs. The FDEs identified the

writers with a 98% accuracy rate (Durina and Caligiuri, 2009).

3. Twins were the subjects of the study *On the Discriminability of the Handwriting of Twins* by Dr. Srihari (Srihari, 2008). A computer program was used to discriminate the handwriting of twins and non-twins. The computer program was able to differentiate the twins with a 12.91% error rate and a 3.7% error rate for non-twins. The computer outperformed laypeople, but not FDEs.

4. A New Zealand study (Boot, 1998) titled *An Investigation into the Degree of Similarity in the Handwriting of Identical and Fraternal Twins in New Zealand* found that FDEs could distinguish the handwriting of 95 sets of twins.

5. A Canadian study (Gamble, 1980) titled *The Handwriting of Identical Twins* found that the handwriting of 58 sets of twins could be differentiated.

6. *A Statistical Study of Handwritings by Twins and Other Persons of Multiple Births* (Beacom, 1960) found that with sufficient known writings, the 50 sets of twins could be differentiated.

7. *Lineup: The Reliability of Examinations Involving Multiple Writers* (Parrett and Szabo, 2003) used 1,000 known writing samples from 1,000 individuals with one questioned document. All FDEs identified the correct writer in each test.

8. In *The Nicola Brazier Murder: The Role of Handwriting in a Large-Scale Investigation* (Harvey and Mitchell, 1973) the FDE was able to identify the writer of a check that was evidence in a homicide investigation. Known writings from 1,046 men were submitted in the case.

9. *The Large Scale Searching of Handwriting Samples* (Baxendale and Renshaw, 1979) was another homicide case. Handwritten notes that related to a kidnapping were found in a stolen car. The search for the writer of the notes was performed by an FDE. Handwriting samples from 600,000 individuals were examined in the case, ultimately leading to an identification of the murderer.

10. *A Review of Handwriting Search Cases as an Indicator of the Individuality of Handwriting* (Welch, 1999) describes the work of FDEs in four criminal cases in the United Kingdom related to handwriting identification. FDEs in the four cases were able to successfully identify the writers of questioned documents involving approximately 1,000, 1,300, 100,000, and 600,000 writers. The cases demonstrate strong evidence for the individuality of handwriting.

11. In *The Uniqueness of Handwriting* (Vastrick, 1998), a survey gathered data from 91 FDEs regarding the uniqueness of individual handwriting in their experience. Handwriting studies of a variety of

aspects of handwriting were considered along with the experience of FDEs to support the principle that handwriting is individual.

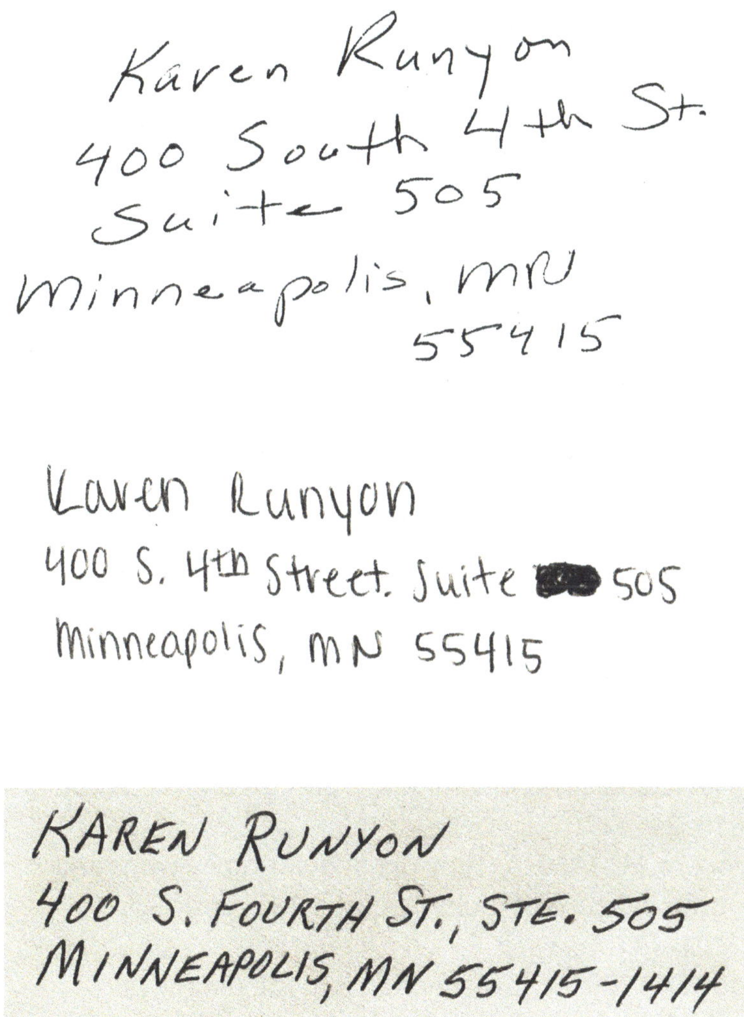

FIGURE 4.1 Handwriting samples from three different writers.

12. In *Case Report: The Individuality of Handwriting Demonstrated Through the Field Screening of 1000 Writers* (Shiver, 1996), questioned checks were compared to 1,000 postal locator cards and other postal documents by an FDE. Only one known postal card had significant similarities with the handwriting on the questioned checks. Later in the investigation, latent prints of the same suspect whose handwriting was identified were developed and identified on the questioned checks.

13. Forensic Information System for Handwriting (FISH) is a database used by federal and international law enforcement agencies. The database contains more than 110,000 writers. No two persons have the same handwriting characteristics in the current group.

Figure 4.1 illustrates several handwriting examples demonstrating handwriting individuality.

References

Baxendale, D., Renshaw, I.D., 1979. The large scale searching of handwriting samples. J. Forensic Sci. Soc. 19, 245–251.

Beacom, M., 1960. A study of handwriting by twins and other persons of multiple births. J. Forensic Sci. 5, 121–131.

Boot, D., 1998. An investigation into the degree of similarity in the handwriting of identical and fraternal twins in New Zealand. J. Am. Soc. Questioned Document Exam. 1 (2), 70–81.

Durina, M., Caligiuri, M., 2009. The determination of authorship from a homogenous group of writers. J. Am. Soc. Questioned Document Exam. 12 (2), 1–14.
Gamble, D., 1980. The handwriting of identical twins. Canadian Soc. Forensic Sci. J. 13, 11–30.
Harvey, R., Mitchell, M., 1973. The Nicole Brazier murder: the role of handwriting in a large-scale investigation. J. Forensic Sci. Soc. 13, 157–168.
Hilton, O., 1963. Some basic rules for the identification of handwriting. Medicine, Science and the Law. Br. Acad. Forensic Sci. 3, 107–117.
Osborn, A., 1929. Questioned Documents, Second ed. Nelson-Hall, Chicago, p. 30.
Parrett, D., Szabo, G., 2003. Lineup: the reliability of examinations involving multiple writers. J. Am. Soc. Questioned Document Exam. 6 (2), 82–84.
Shiver, F., 1996. Prepared for the 54th Annual Conference of the American Society of Questioned Document Examiners, Washington, D.C., August 24–28, 1996.
Srihari, S., Cha, S., Arora, H., Lee, S., 2002. Individuality of handwriting. J. Forensic Sci. 47 (4), 856–872.
Srihari, S., Huang, C., Srinivasan, H., 2008. On the discriminability of the handwriting of twins. J. Forensic Sci. 53 (2), 430–446.
Vastrick, T., 1998. The uniqueness of handwriting. J. Am. Soc. Questioned Document Exam. 1 (1), 4–7.
Welch, J., 1999. A review of handwriting search cases as an indicator of the individuality of handwriting. Int. J. Forensic Document Exam 5, 283–284.

Basic Methodology

Chapter Outline

Forensic Document Examination. http://dx.doi.org/10.1016/B978-0-12-416693-6.00005-9

The whole of science is nothing more than a refinement of everyday thinking.
(Albert Einstein, Physics and Reality, 1936)

Methodology in Forensic Document Examination

What is your methodology? This is a common question posed to an FDE in a pretrial conference with an attorney. Examinations are complex. The evidence submitted for examination and comparison may range from a questioned signature on a will to ten pages of hand printing in an anonymous threatening letter case. Though the evidence and examinations may be complex, we strive for simple descriptions of our methods. FDEs articulate their consistent methodology in slightly different ways. The scientific method is always applied to questioned document cases. This is an approach that begins with complete neutrality and considers the questioned evidence based on the extensive background knowledge on the subject. Significant individualizing characteristics between questioned and known documents lead to an identification. Significant differences observed between questioned and known documents support elimination. Today FDEs use simple descriptions of the comparison of questioned with known using appropriate lighting, magnification, and time to explain their methodology. Another way to explain the complex methodology of handwriting comparison is the ACE method.

ACE Method

ACE is an acronym originated by the Canadian FDE, Roy Huber. ACE represents: Analysis, Comparison, and Evaluation. He used it in his article published in *The Criminal Law Quarterly* (Huber, 1959). He described the process of identification in the following way.

There are three distinct stages in establishing the identity of any person or thing through which the forensic scientist must pass, consciously or otherwise, in the course of his examination:

1. *Analysis. The "unknown" item must be classified according to its properties or characteristics. These properties may be directly observable, measurable, or implied, but they are the parts which make up the whole.*

2. *Comparison. Stripped of its pictorial effects, its subjective disillusions, and now seen for what it really is, a comparison is made of the properties of the item found through analysis with the known of recorded properties of others whose identity is unquestioned.*

3. *Evaluation. It is not sufficient that the comparison disclose similarities or dissimilarities in any of the characteristic properties of knowns and unknowns. Each property will have a certain value for identification purposes, determined chiefly by its relative frequency of occurrence. The weight or significance of each must be considered.*

Latent print examiners use the ACE method to describe their methodology today. David Ashbaugh (Ashbaugh, 1999) applied the ACE method to fingerprints.

Even earlier than Huber, FDE Albert S. Osborn can be credited with the idea of ACE in his book *Questioned Documents* (Osborn, 1910) where he states, "...the investigation of documents presents problems which in the main are to be solved by the study, comparison and interpretation of that which in some form is actually present before the court."

FDE Peter Tytell reworked the ASTM Standard Guide for Examination of Handwritten Items E2290-07a (ASTM, 2013) in the framework of the ACE concept. This developed into a handout used by the American Board of Forensic Document Examiners (ABFDE) (Tytell, 2013). The following is one page of the ABFDE handout:

> *Procedure for Examination of Handwritten items*
>
> *(Broken out according to the ACE concept (Analysis, Comparison, Evaluation) of forensic examinations)*
>
> ***Analysis***
>
> ***For Questioned***
>
> *Original or non-original.*
>
> > *If non-original, evaluate quality:*

Significant details reproduced with sufficient clarity for comparison?

Does writing appear distorted?

Is writing natural?

Evaluate Questioned for:

Type of writing

Internal consistency

Range of variation

Presence (or absence) of Individualizing characteristics.

For Known

Original or non-original.

If non-original, evaluate quality:

Significant details reproduced with sufficient clarity for comparison?

Does writing appear distorted?

Is writing natural?

Evaluate Known for:

Type of writing

Internal consistency

Range of variation

Presence (or absence) of

Individualizing characteristics.

Comparison

Evaluate comparability of the bodies of writing.

Side-by-side comparison of comparable portions of the bodies of writing.

Look for differences, absent characters, or similarities.

Evaluation

Evaluate sufficiency of the quantity of writing compared.

Analyze, compare, and evaluate the individualizing characteristics and other potentially significant features in the comparable portions of the bodies of writing.

Evaluate the similarities, differences, and limitations.

Determine their significance individually and in combination.

Reach a determination based on results of the above analysis, comparisons, and evaluations. Report accordingly.

Elements of Writing in Forensic Document Examination

The ACE concept is a simple framework to describe the methodology of FDE in elemental terms. More specific features considered in the examination of questioned handwriting are described in ASTM Standard E2290-07a (ASTM, 2013) in Note 6:

Among the features to be considered are elements of the writing such as abbreviation; alignment; arrangement, formatting, and positioning; capitalization; connectedness and disconnectedness; cross strokes and dots, diacritics and punctuation; direction of strokes; disguise; embellishments; formation; freedom of execution; handedness; legibility; line quality; method of production; pen hold and pen position; overall pressure and patterns of pressure emphasis; proportion; simplification; size; skill; slant or slope; spacing; speed; initial, connecting, and terminal strokes; system; tremor; type of writing; and range of variation.

Other features such as lifts, stops and hesitations of the writing instrument; patching and retouching;

slow, drawn quality of the line; unnatural tremor; and guide lines of various forms should be evaluated when present.

Other Ways to Articulate FDE Methodology

ASTM E444-09

Another way to articulate the methodology of forensic document examination exists in another ASTM standard, the Standard Guide for the Scope of Work of Forensic Document Examiners E444-09 (ASTM, 2013):

> *4.4 Questions about documents are answered through the application of knowledge, skill, experience, training, (Guide E2388), or education specific to forensic document examination as well as from a number of other fields, such as the physical sciences, mathematics, language studies, and the like. The field of interest includes manufacturing processes and the materials that go into the production of documents, as well as the methods, machines, instruments, and human agencies by which the parts of documents are formed or brought together.*

David Ellen

In his book *Scientific Examination of Documents: Methods and Techniques* (Ellen, 2006), David Ellen suggests that evidence must be weighed considering the background knowledge on the subject. This knowledge is gained through analytical study of vast numbers of handwriting cases. He advises that the hypothesis that two writings were written by one person must be tested against the similarities and variations observed in the population considered.

Dan Purdy

In his chapter *Identification of Handwriting* in the book *Scientific Examination of Questioned Documents, Second Edition* (Purdy, 2006), Dan Purdy describes identification of handwriting based on a substantial combination of distinctive habit characteristics in both the questioned and known handwriting. The questioned and known writings must also exhibit the same range of natural variation. Identification of the writer of a document in question requires the assessment of letters and letter combinations and qualities more difficult to measure, like line quality, pressure patterns, spacing, skill level, and freedom of movement.

William Riordan et al.

In Chapter 9, *Forensic Document Examination,* from the book *Forensic Science: Current Issues, Future Directions* (Riordan et al., 2013), the methodology of forensic document examination is articulated emphasizing application of the scientific method to questioned document cases. An objective evaluation of questioned and known writings is performed using a neutral approach. The quality and comparability of the evidence directly determines the opinion in the case. Known standards must be contemporaneous, collected in sufficient quantity, and must reproduce the material in question. Individual letters in a questioned document are directly compared to counterparts in the known sample using a side-by-side comparison. Features in the questioned writing are then evaluated to assess whether they fit within the range of variation in the known writing sample. Identification is based on a broad range of characteristics in the writing.

Natural Variation in Handwriting

Consideration of natural variation in handwriting is part of the methodology of FDEs. Natural variation consists of typical small changes in repeated writing of the same material by one person. Figure 5.1 is an example of natural variation in the writing of one person. We expect to see natural variation because no one writes exactly the same way twice. This is because people are not writing machines and

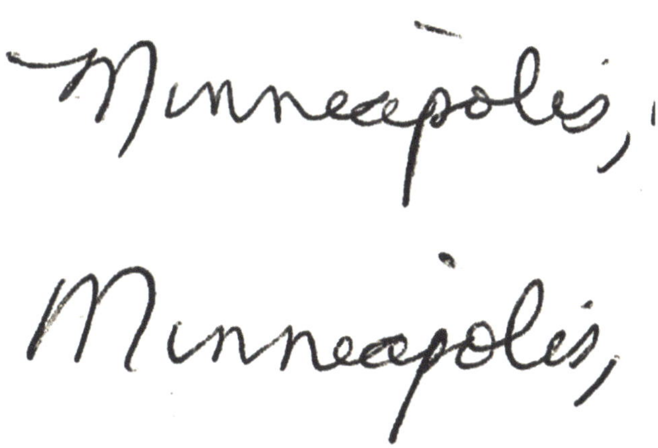

FIGURE 5.1 Natural variation occurs in the uppercase "M" in "Minneapolis" of one writer.

handwriting is a dynamic and complex activity. Handwriting is a combination of the coordination of fingers, hand, arm, eyes, and brain. Natural variation in one person's handwriting may result from the speed of the writing on a particular occasion and formal writing contrasted with informal writing. The range of natural variation may be limited, and mainly consistent or lacking in uniformity, depending on the skill and writing ability of each person. Variation between two writers is more distinct than that within the writing of one person. Variations between two writers are called "differences" by FDEs. Figure 5.2 is an example of "Milwaukee, WI" written by two different writers. The handwriting on greeting cards from friends and family are easily distinguished and recognized by the layman.

Recent research with the software program Write-On2 applied the statistical function of the program to specifically assess natural variation in handwriting. According to Lindblom (Lindblom, 2013):

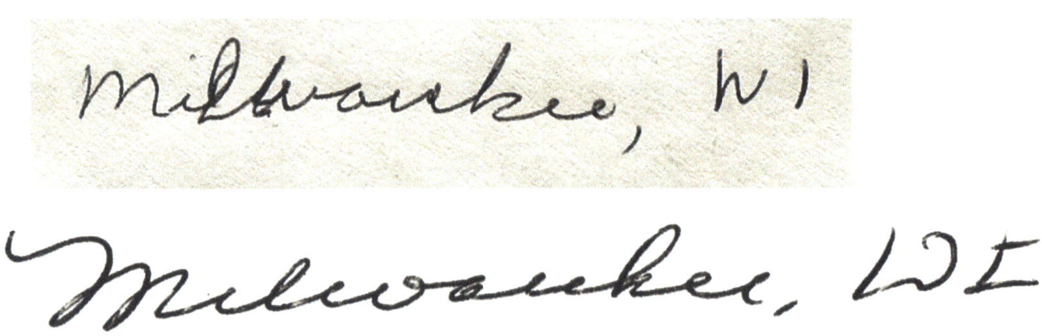

FIGURE 5.2 "Milwaukee, WI" written by two different writers.

Write-On 2 software is a database that assists forensic document examiners in the collection, dissection and analysis of handwriting. Occurrence Charts that show all instances of a particular character or combination of characters are generated through sophisticated searches. Within the program, Word and Segment Indexes are available from which searches can be launched. Included in the indices are columns showing the number of occurrences in both the questioned and sample material. This statistical information is very helpful in assessing natural variation in handwriting. For example, one can readily determine how many occurrences of a given letter combination appear in the documents and weigh findings accordingly. From the Occurrence Charts the FDE is directed to the location of a given character within the original documents. Unlike doing traditional side-by-side comparisons, the FDE does not have to be concerned with the possibility that one or more examples of a letter may have been missed within the questioned and/or sample material.

Conclusion

FDEs articulate a common methodology in slightly different ways. The ACE (Analysis, Comparison, and Evaluation) method is a convenient way to explain the details in our examination process that we perform thoughtfully yet automatically. The application of the scientific method to the examination of questioned documents is characterized by objectivity and a systematic comparison of questioned with known.

References

Ashbaugh, D.R., 1999. Quantitative-qualitative friction ridge analysis. CRC Press, Taylor & Francis Group, Boca Raton, Florida.

ASTM International. ASTM Standard, 2013. Standard guide for examination of handwritten items. E2290–07a. West Conshohocken, Pennsylvania.

ASTM International. ASTM Standard, 2013. Standard guide for scope of the work of forensic document examiners. E444–09. West Conshohocken, Pennsylvania.

Ellen, D., 2006. Scientific Examination of Documents: Methods and Techniques, Third ed. CRC Press, Taylor & Francis Group, Boca Raton, Florida.

Huber, R., 1959. Expert witnesses: in defense of expert witnesses in general and of document examiners in particular. Criminal Law Quarterly 2 (3), 274–295.

Lindblom, B., June 4-5, 2013. Using the Statistical Functions of Write-On 2 Software to Assess Natural Variation in Handwriting. Presentation at the Measurement Science & Standards in Forensic Handwriting Analysis conference sponsored by NIST in Gaithersburg, Maryland.

Osborn, A., 1910. Questioned Documents. Lawyers' Co-operative Publishing Co, Rochester, New York.

Purdy, D.C., 2006. Identification of Handwriting. In: Kelly, J.S. and Lindblom, B.S. (Eds.), Scientific Examination of Questioned Documents, Second edition. CRC, Taylor & Francis Group, Boca Raton, FL, pp. 47–74.

Riordan, W.M., Gustafson, J.A., Fitzgerald, M.P., Lewis, J.A., 2013. Forensic document examination. In: Ubelaker, D.H. (Ed.), Forensic Science: Current Issues, Future Directions. Wiley-Blackwell, Chichester, West Sussex, UK, pp. 224–251.

Tytell, P., personal communication. 2013.

Instrumentation

Chapter Outline

Forensic Document Examination. http://dx.doi.org/10.1016/B978-0-12-416693-6.00006-0

That great, growing engine of change – technology.
(Alvin Toffler, Future Shock, 1970)

Scientific examination of questioned documents requires basic instrumentation specialized for the FDE. Detailed examination of signatures begins with lighting and magnification. A stereo microscope is applied to most disputed handwriting, hand printing, and commercial printing cases. Details revealing a simulated signature are discovered with a camera attached to a stereo microscope or a handheld digital microscope. Alterations to medical records are visualized with an imaging instrument like the Video Spectral Comparator. Illumination with a light panel allows forms to be overlaid to observe consistency of format and watermarks on paper to shine forth. Latent indented writing on an anonymous letter is developed with an ESDA. Scanners, personal computers, imaging software, and cameras help construct court charts that illustrate our opinions. Specialized grids detect insertions in typewritten documents or computer-generated documents.

Stereo Microscope

A binocular stereo microscope forms the core of vital instruments for the FDE. Magnification of 6–50× encompasses the usual range used by FDEs. Illumination from a fiber optic light with two goose neck light sources can be flexibly positioned to view documents from above or with grazing light from the side of a document.

FIGURE 6.1 Stereo microscope with fiber optic light source. *(Photograph by Lisa Gordee)*

Figure 6.1 shows a stereo microscope with a fiber optic light source.

Magnifiers

Magnifiers from 3.5–7× enlarge the details of handwriting, typewriting, and printing methods for FDEs. Some magnifiers are framed on small stands and others are handheld. Figure 6.2 shows an array of common magnifiers used in questioned document examination.

Light Panels

Light panels or light boxes consisting of two fluorescent lamps allow FDEs to view documents with a strong transmitted light source. Light panels illustrate watermarks on paper, which can provide dating evidence on the paper. Information develops from

FIGURE 6.2 Magnifiers used by forensic document examiners.

overlaying two documents to determine consistency of format of computer-generated documents or the presence of alterations to documents.

MiScope

The MiScope is a small handheld digital microscope. Instead of the conventional eyepieces used in stereo microscopes, the MiScope plugs into the USB port of a laptop computer and is focused with a sliding control on the side of the instrument. The range of magnification is from 12–140×. Images appear on the computer screen. Photomicrographs can be saved, printed, and attached to reports to illustrate characteristics of the handwriting like tremor, pen lifts, and blunt beginning and ending strokes. The MiScope illustrates the characteristics of simulated signatures, and overwritten and altered documents. Figure 6.3 shows the MiScope in use.

FIGURE 6.3 MiScope. *(Photograph by Lisa Gordee)*

Video Spectral Comparators

A video camera, light source, and filters, including the visible, ultraviolet, and near infrared part of the electromagnetic spectrum constitute the elementary parts of video spectral comparator imaging instruments. G.B. Richards described the basic principles of the early technology (Richards, 1977). The video spectral comparator models VSC 40/HD in Figure 6.4 and the VSC 6000/HS in Figure 6.5 are two examples of this technology. These instruments help FDEs differentiate visually similar inks, detect alterations, and decipher obliterations.

Hyperspectral Imaging

"Multispectral and hyperspectral imaging collect images of an object in a series of spectral windows" (Liang, 2011). Hyperspectral imaging is differentiated from multispectral imaging by resolution (Ostrum, 2006).

FIGURE 6.4 VSC 40/HD made by Foster and Freeman.

FIGURE 6.5 VSC6000/HS made by Foster and Freeman.

Multispectral imaging (MSI) collects images from specific areas of the electromagnetic spectrum. The definition of multispectral imaging may vary depending on whom or what discipline is defining it. Multispectral imaging has from 4 to 20 color channels, with a grayscale image having 1 wavelength or color channel, a Red–Green–Blue image 3 wavelengths for each pixel, and CYMK 4 color channels. Hyperspectral imaging (HSI) consists of many more than 20 bands of spectral data for each pixel. In both MSI and HSI, the images are stacked up to form an image cube. The size depends on the number of wavelengths used (Stephens, 2013).

Initial applications of MSI and HSI were designed for remote sensing used in planetary science, astronomy, and many other areas (Liang, 2011). Since the 1990s, cultural heritage and art conservation have applied MSI and HSI to that work (Liang, 2011).

The Library of Congress hosted a workshop on HSI for FDEs in 2013 in Washington, D.C. HSI enjoys the advantage of being a remote, non-destructive spectroscopic technique with applications to cultural and forensic cases. HSI may recover faded or obliterated writing, identify pigments by their spectral signature, and reveal watermarks. Dr. Fanella France of the Library of Congress Preservation Research and Testing Division explained the application of HSI to the Pierre L'Enfant Plan of Washington, D.C. (1791) in her paper "Advanced Image Analysis for the Preservation of Cultural Heritage" (France et al., 2010).

Two commercial HSI instruments designed specifically for FDEs are available: the VSC 6000/HS made by Foster and Freeman (Figure 6.5), and the HSI Examiner 200 QD Hyperspectral Imaging System from Chem Image. These systems offer the possibility to expand the range of ink discrimination for FDEs. HSI systems are not yet in general use by FDEs because of the high cost and need to store very large image files.

Electrostatic Detection Devices

Latent indented writing on paper can be visualized with an electrostatic detection device (EDD). Foster and Freeman introduced the Electrostatic Detection Apparatus (ESDA) in 1968 (Purdy, 1999). The Indentation Materializer Electrostatic Detection Device (IMEDD) was produced by Kinderprint and sold as the Docubox (Purdy, 1999).

Every FDE needs an EDD in order to process documents to develop latent indented impressions. These indented impressions occur when a writing instrument forms impressions on a substrate below the sheet that originally overlaid the document. Typical cases that require an EDD include: anonymous letters, bank robbery notes, and medical records.

EDDs consist of a humidifying chamber, transparent imaging film, cascade developer, a document platen, vacuum pump, coronal wand, and fixing film.

Photography and Imaging

Photography and scanning of all questioned and known documents are necessary to capture details important to the case and record in a general way all of the evidence submitted. Study charts may then be constructed from the questioned and known materials. These study charts capture the main elements of a case in a nutshell for review and demonstration.

A digital single-lens reflex camera like the Nikon D5100 (or equivalent) and additional high performance micro lenses like the AF-S Micro-Nikkor 60mm f/2.8G ED lens capture details of questioned documents for the FDE. The camera is mounted over the document with a Quadrapod sold by Forensic Imaging, Inc. A Quadrapod provides a steady base for the camera with one more leg than a tripod. It helps capture indented writing when used with a grazing light source, and general handwriting, typewriting, and disputed printing method details.

Recording details of interest on questioned documents usually begins with high-quality scans. A scanner like the Epson Perfection V500 Photo (or equivalent) assists FDEs in recording evidence electronically for making study charts, illustrations, and court charts. Adobe Photoshop CS6 or similar imaging software allows enhancement of images and the construction of clear enlargements of questioned documents. Study charts, illustrations of evidence, and court charts can be printed out with a high-quality inkjet printer like the Epson Stylus Photo R1800 or similar printer.

Specialized Grids

Specialized grids help the FDE detect alignment defects and insertions in typewritten documents and computer-generated documents. Rectilinear glass test plates designed by Lyman Nichols were available in 10 pitch pica (2.54 mm) and 12 pitch elite (2.11666 mm) or in film copies (Tytell, 1986). Today computer-generated grids printed on transparent film serve to help the FDE detect insertions and alignment defects in computer-generated documents.

References

France, F., Christens-Barry, W., Toth, M., Boydston, K., 2010. Advanced image analysis for the preservation of cultural heritage. Proc. SPIE 7531, Comput. Vision and Image Analysis of Art, 75310dE (February 16, 2010); doi:10.1117/12.839000, pp. 1–12.

Liang, H., 2011. Advances in multispectral and hyperspectral imaging for archaeology and art conservation. Appl. Physics A 2 (106), 309–323.

Ostrum, B., 2006. Application of hyperspectral imaging to forensic document examination problems. J. Am. Soc. Questioned Document Exam. 2 (9), 85–93.

Purdy, D., 1999. A method for determining the condition of an ESDA or IMEDD. J. Am. Soc. Questioned Document Exam. 2 (2), 97–101.

Richards, G., 1977. The application of electronic video techniques to infrared and ultraviolet examinations. J. Forensic Sci. 1 (22), 53–60.

Stephens, J., personal communication 2013.

Tytell, P., September 21–25, 1986. Measurement grids and the contemporary document examiner. Presentation at the American Society of Questioned Document Examiners Annual Meeting in Savannah, Georgia.

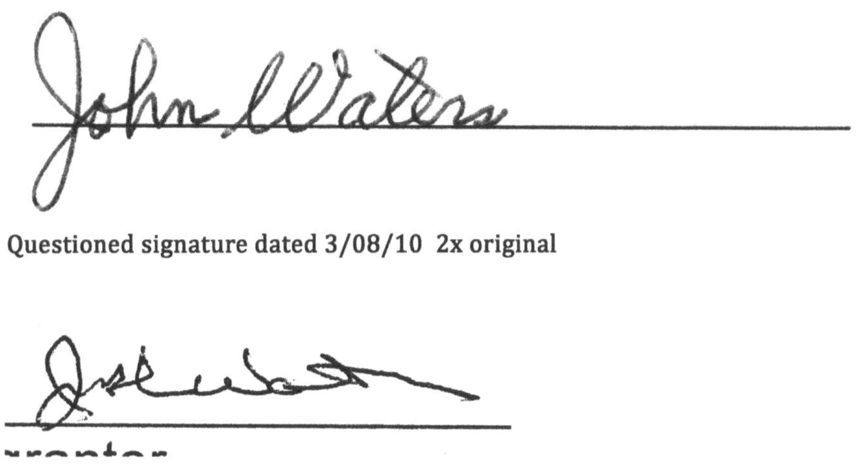

CHAPTER 7

Questioned signature dated 3/08/10 2x original

K1-22 Document notarized by Arthur Czaja dated 5/18/10 2x copy

Case Examples

Chapter Outline

Forensic Document Examination. http://dx.doi.org/10.1016/B978-0-12-416693-6.00007-2

That is the essence of science: ask an impertinent question, and you are on the way to the pertinent answer.

(Jacob Bronowski, The Ascent of Man, 1973)

Introduction

FDEs examine a plethora of cases throughout their careers. In crime laboratories, typical questioned document cases include: forged checks, threatening letters, bank robbery notes, school bomb threats, graffiti, nomination papers, tax forms, anonymous letters, and suicide notes. Civil cases worked by FDEs in private practice include: disputed signatures on mortgage documents, wills, medical records alteration cases, contracts, deeds, loan documents, change of beneficiary forms, receipts, partnership agreements, noncompete agreements, anonymous letters in the work place, log entries, power of attorney, and health care forms.

My experience consists of both criminal cases submitted to crime laboratories and civil and criminal cases submitted to me in private practice. Cases described in this chapter fall mostly on the civil side. Several criminal cases will be discussed only in the abstract, without any specific details about the persons involved in the cases.

John Waters Will Case

In 2011 I received an Illinois disputed will case. The questioned document was an original three-page will.

The questioned signature appeared on page one of the questioned will. The known writing sample consisted of 38 signatures of John Waters. The requested examination was to determine whether the questioned "John Waters" signature on the Item Q1a will was written by the John Waters. Examinations conducted consisted of visual and microscopic examinations of the questioned and known signatures and then comparison of the questioned with the known signatures in the case.

The analysis assessed features including line quality, writing style, alignment, connecting strokes, degree of angularity and roundness, beginning and ending strokes, letter design, connections and disconnections of letters, proportions of letters, relative heights of letters, size, slant, spacing, and speed of the writing. The comparison disclosed a few similarities and significant differences. The differences observed in Q1a are listed below:

- Different shape of the upper loop of the J.
- Blunt beginning stroke of the J.
- Tremor at the lower loop of the o.
- Different design of the arch of the h.
- The n is slowly written.
- The ending stroke of the n is a blunt retraced stroke.

- The beginning stroke of the W is a blunt retraced stroke.
- The ending loop of the W exhibits hesitation at the top.
- The ending loop of the W ends with a blunt stroke.
- The a begins with a blunt stroke.
- The design of the a is different from those in the known writings.
- The r is a different design from the known writings.
- The r exhibits a hesitation point at the top of the letter.
- The ending s is written slowly with a blunt ending stroke.

Based on examination of the questioned signature and comparison with the known signatures, it was my opinion that the writer of K1-1–K1-38 (John Waters) did not write the questioned "John Waters" signature on the will (Item Q1a). The questioned signature on the will was a simulation of a genuine signature of John Waters.

A study chart created at case submission showed the questioned signature on the will and all 38 known signatures of John Waters submitted for comparison. I attached this to the report along with a chart constructed with the questioned signature enlarged 2× and five known signatures of John Waters also enlarged 2×. The five known signatures were chosen because they were contemporaneous with the questioned signature. The questioned signature on the will was dated 3/08/10. The five known signatures were dated in 2009 and 2010.

At the trial in 2013, my report was not introduced. I testified about my comparison with only the five contemporaneous known signatures that I used to construct the 2× court chart. I also used five mini charts to demonstrate the differences between the questioned signature on the will and the known signatures of John Waters. This was not my choice, but a litigation strategy for focusing the judge's attention on one signature pair at a time. I usually juxtapose the questioned signature at the top of the chart and arrange four or five known signatures below it. This strategy of presenting the judge with one questioned and one known signature at a time can be seen in charts shown in Figures 7.1–7.3. The judge appreciated the comparisons of the questioned signature on the will with one contemporaneous known signature on each chart. The judge ruled that the will was a forgery.

Medical Records Case

In 2011 I received a medical records case. The doctor was accused of altering three medical records of a patient with a severe wound. The requested examination was to determine whether certain numerals on

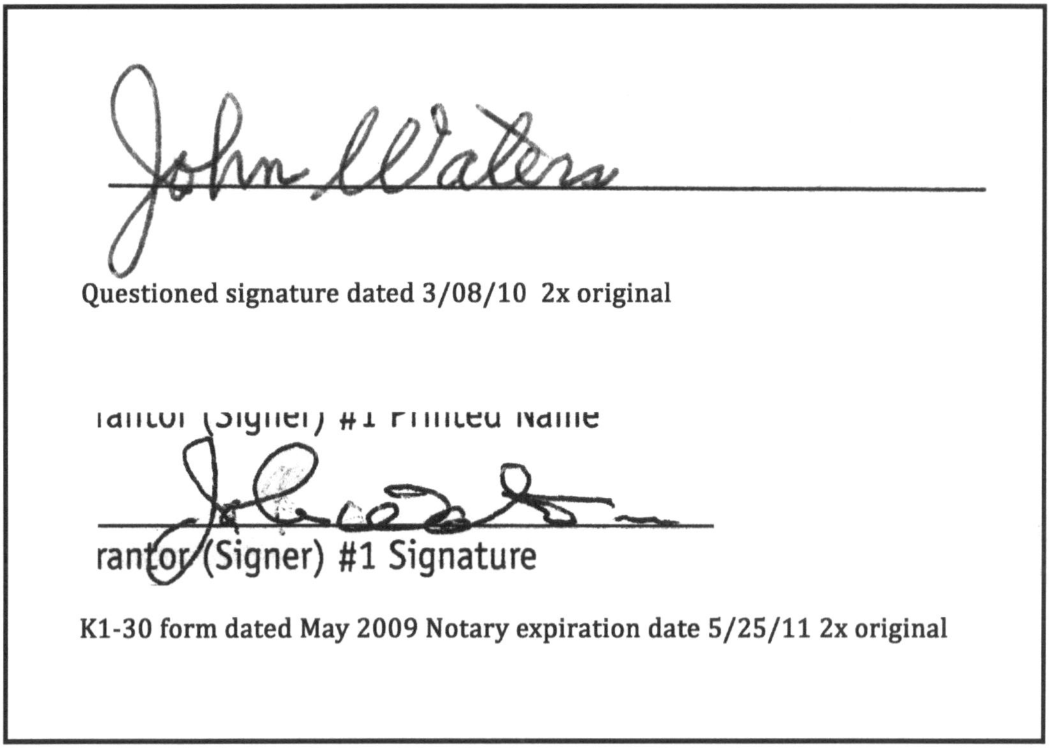

FIGURE 7.1 John Waters Chart 2 shows the questioned signature on the top and one known signature below it. Both signatures are enlarged 2x.

the three pages of a medical record were altered by overwriting. The allegation was that the numbers that represented the sizes of the wound in centimeters and the stages of the wound represented with Roman numerals were changed to make it look as if the patient entered care at the treatment facility with more severe wounds rather than developing the severe wounds after admission to the treatment facility.

The questioned writing on the three pages of medical records was examined visually, microscopically, and

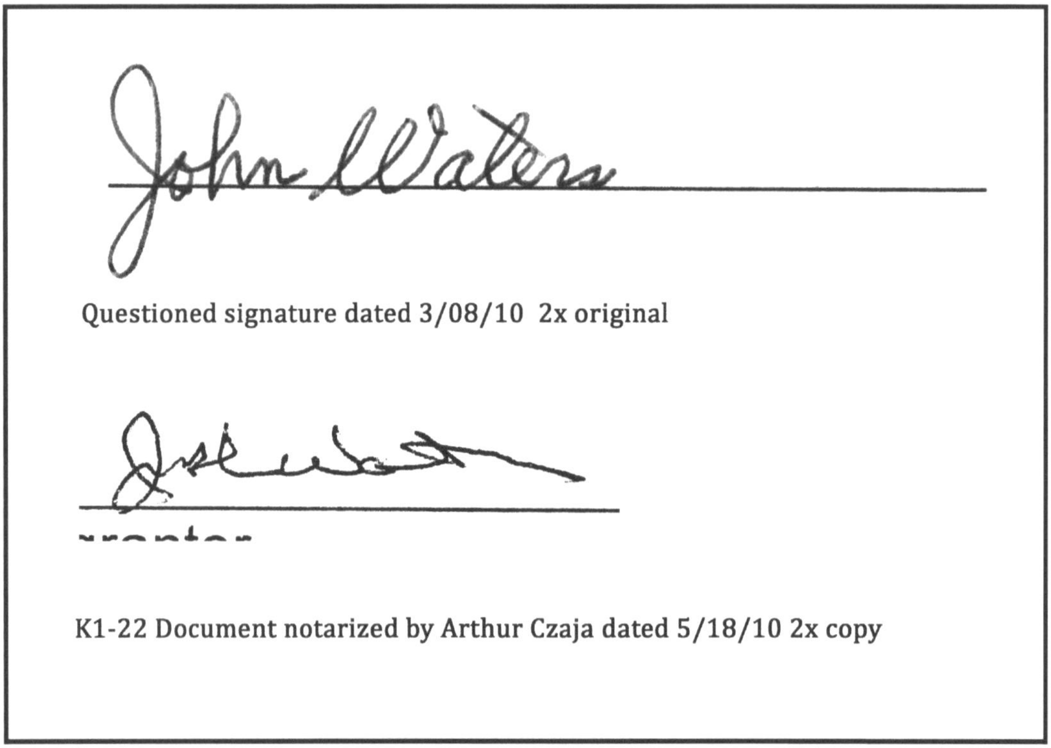

FIGURE 7.2 John Waters Chart 4 shows the questioned signature on the top and the one known signature below it. Both signatures are enlarged 2x.

instrumentally for the presence of alterations. Based on examination of the questioned numerals on the medical records, it was my opinion that overwriting was observed on two of the three pages of the medical records. No alterations were observed on one of the questioned medical records. I observed 12 alterations on Q1 and five alterations on Q3. Figure 7.4 represents a mini chart of a 2× scan of the altered numeral "IV" and a 40× digital microscope photo of the same numeral. The original numeral written on the record read "II"; this was overwritten with black ballpoint pen ink that was a

Questioned signature dated 3/08/10 2x original

K1-33 Illinois ID card dated 1/06/10 2x copy

FIGURE 7.3 John Waters Chart 5 shows the questioned signature on the top and the one known signature below it. Both signatures are enlarged 2x.

slightly different color from the original writing. The overwriting changed stage II to stage IV.

Figure 7.5 shows an image of this same "IV" numeral in an infrared luminescent image from the VSC4 instrument. The overwriting "V" darkened and was separated from the underwriting "II" that luminesced.

Original Contract Case

I received a case in 2013 from a lawyer who asked me to determine whether two contracts were originals or

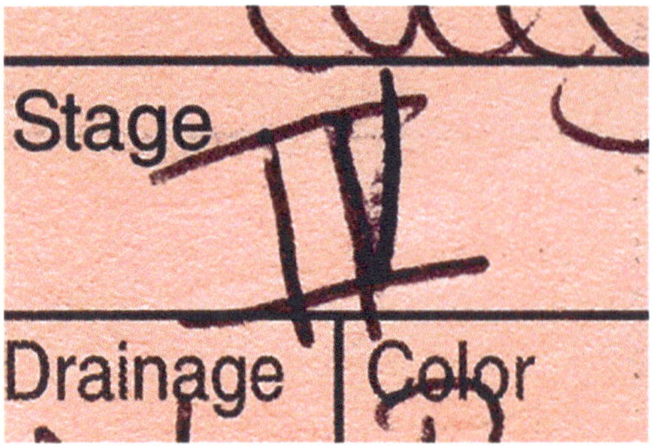

Q1 IV color scan 2x

Q1 IV digital microscope image

FIGURE 7.4 Mini chart of a 2x scan of the altered numeral "IV" and a digital microscope image of the same numeral.

copies. The other side of the case said that the documents were not original, but rather copies. A similar case was submitted to me in 2012. That case went to court. I testified about the characteristics of original

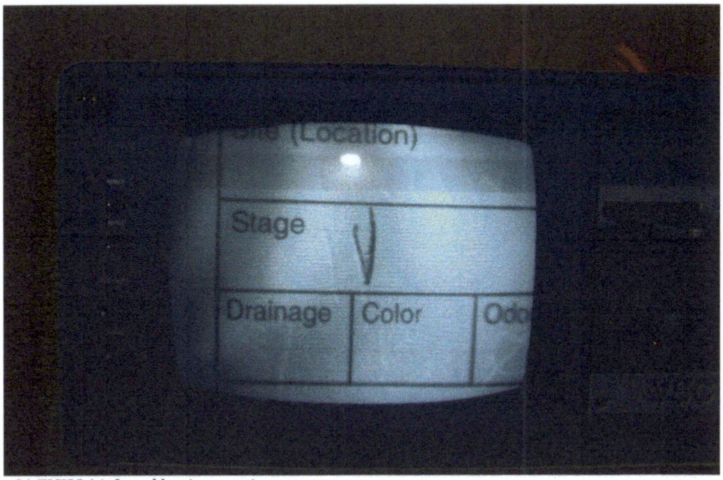

Q1 IV VSC 4 infrared luminescent image

FIGURE 7.5 Image of "IV" numeral in an infrared luminescent image from the VSC4 instrument.

ballpoint pen ink and compared it to the characteristics of toner on paper in photocopiers and laser printers and inkjet printing on paper.

A stereo microscope revealed the characteristics of signatures written with black ballpoint pen ink on one contract and black ballpoint pen ink and black aqueous ink on the second contract. Each form was created with a color inkjet printer. I took photomicrographs of portions of the ballpoint pen ink signatures and addresses on the two questioned documents. I used an Olympus SZ 40 stereo microscope with an Olympus Camedia Digital Camera C-4040 Zoom 4.1 Megapixel mounted on it to capture photomicrographs of the inks on the two questioned documents. Figure 7.6 shows two examples of photomicrographs from two of the signatures on one of the questioned contracts produced with black ballpoint pen ink. The properties of ballpoint pen ink are visible in the photomicrographs. The top image

FIGURE 7.6 Photomicrographs of signatures written with black ballpoint pen ink.

shows the stain glass window effect of ballpoint pen ink as it partially covers the paper substrate with gaps and some non-inked areas. The second partial signature, also written with ballpoint pen, exhibited striation patterns that often occur in ballpoint pens (Lewis, 2003).

I also captured portions of the features of the ballpoint pen signatures and aqueous ink signatures with a MiScope digital microscope. In this case, the photomicrographs produced with a digital camera mounted on the Olympus stereo microscope produced superior images.

Irene V. Vander Zee Will Case

In 2011 I received a disputed will case in Wisconsin. The evidence consisted of a holographic will written in black ballpoint pen ink dated 5/14/09 and forty known signatures of Irene V. Vander Zee. The known sample consisted of original documents, copies and signatures contemporaneous with the questioned signature. The disputed will left all of Irene V. Vander Zee's possessions to her sister. The requested examination was to determine whether the signature on the disputed will was written by the writer of the known signatures (Irene V. Vander Zee).

The questioned signature on the disputed will was examined visually, microscopically, and instrumentally. The known signatures of Irene V. Vander Zee were examined visually and microscopically and compared to the questioned signature on the disputed will. Figure 7.7 is an example of a chart showing 2× enlargements of the questioned signature on the disputed will and four known signatures from Irene V. Vander Zee for comparison.

Based on examination of the questioned signature and comparison with the known signatures of Irene

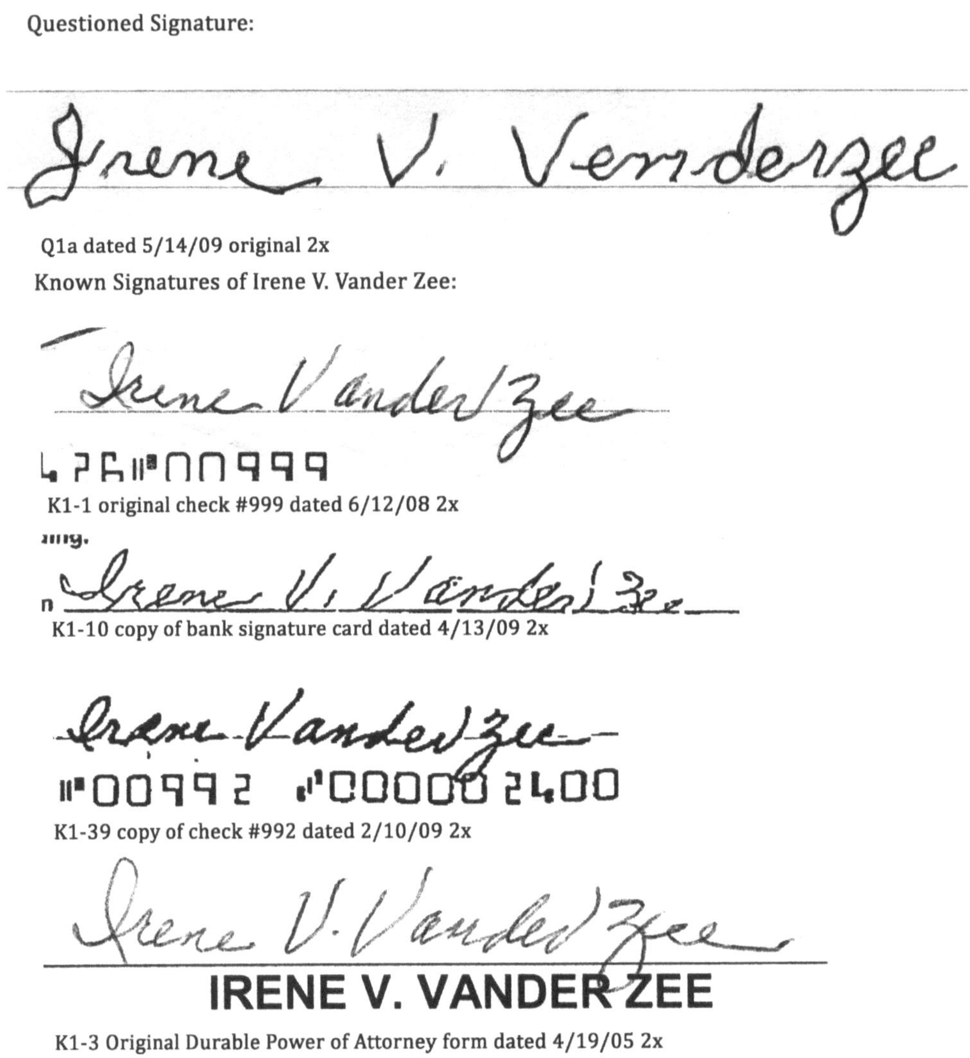

FIGURE 7.7 Chart showing 2x enlargements of the questioned signature on the disputed will and four known signatures from Irene V. Vander Zee for comparison.

V. Vander Zee submitted, it was my opinion that the writer of Items K1-1–K1-40 (Irene V. Vander Zee) did not write the questioned "Irene V. Venderzee" signature on the questioned will.

The visual and microscopic examinations revealed poor line quality with tremor and hesitation in the construction of the questioned signature. The surname in the questioned signature was misspelled. The known signatures had better line quality than the questioned signature. Along with the misspelling, the questioned signature had several pen lifts that were not found in the known samples.

The will was ruled a forgery.

Cases with Low Resolution Images of Checks

Since 2004, Check Clearing for the 21st Century (Check 21) legislation in the United States allows checks to be cleared through the banking system electronically. Images of checks move swiftly through the banks rather than the old system of transferring paper checks. Images of checks are captured with scanners. The resolution setting of the scanner and whether checks are scanned in black and white, gray scale, or color determines the amount of detail and clarity of the scanned images. The banks may also reduce or enlarge the size of the checks in the scanning process. Forensic document examiners receive cases with low resolution and reduced sized images of checks provided by banks. The quality of the image may limit the amount of detail available for analysis. Banks could assist FDEs by scanning their checks at a minimum of 300 ppi, in gray scale or in color (Lewis, 2013).

Figure 7.8 shows two checks scanned at different resolutions and settings. The top check was scanned in black and white at 100 ppi. The low resolution and black-and-white setting reduces the quality and clarity of handwriting details in the image. The lower

FIGURE 7.8 The top check was scanned in black and white at 100 ppi. The lower check was scanned using a 24-bit color setting and 300 ppi.

check was scanned using a 24-bit color setting and 300 ppi. The higher resolution and color provides the most detail for examination (Masson, 2012).

Typewriter Defect Case

Two typewritten threatening anonymous letters were received by a small business approximately ten years ago. No suspects were immediately developed in the case. The typewritten questioned documents were examined for indented writing and processed with an Electrostatic Detection Apparatus (ESDA). No indented material of significance was developed with the ESDA. The letters were made with a typewriter using a carbon typewriter ribbon. A typewriter defect was observed in the lowercase "d" which exhibited a nonprint area at the lower right portion of the loop of the "d." Figure 7.9 is an image of the lowercase "d" with a defect. A suspect was eventually developed. The

FIGURE 7.9 Typewriter defect in the lower right portion of the d.

suspect's typewriter ribbon contained the text of one of the questioned threatening letters on it, and the lowercase "d" exhibited the same defect found in the questioned documents. Today, far more documents are generated by computer printers than typewriters, but the occasional typewritten document case is received by FDEs.

Alteration Case

A questioned document was altered by obliteration. A portion of the writing on the document was covered with correction fluid. I was asked to decipher the writing beneath the correction fluid. The questioned document was examined with a stereo microscope, a video spectral comparator, and a light box. The questioned writing was not deciphered using these methods. The writing beneath the correction fluid was deciphered using the film positive setting on a scanner. The Epson Perfection V500 Photo scanner was used by removing the white backing panel on the top lid of the scanner. This revealed the strip where film may be positioned for scanning. The correction fluid obliteration was positioned within the film strip area on the scanner. Levels, brightness and contrast tools on the scanner were used to adjust the image to reveal the writing under the correction fluid. Further image enhancement was made using the levels tool when the image was opened in Adobe Photoshop. Figure 7.10 shows a sample of the type of obliteration received in the alteration case. The top image is a scan of the questioned obliteration in reflective setting on

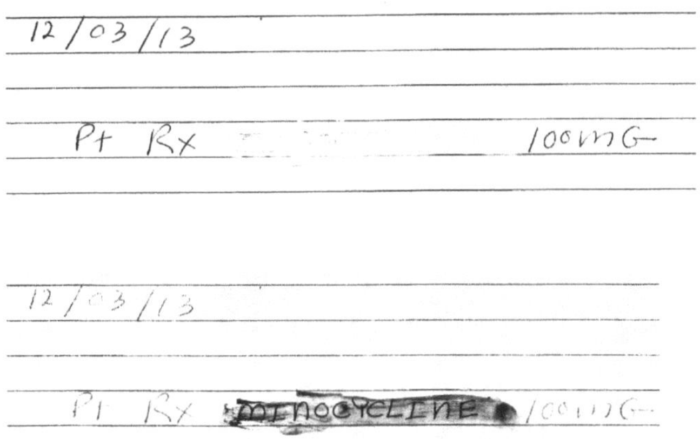

FIGURE 7.10 The top image is a scan of a correction fluid obliteration in reflective setting on the scanner and the lower image is the film positive scan of the same document.

the scanner and the lower image is the film-positive scan of the same document.

Alteration to a Letter

A letter was received as evidence of a planned assault on another person. The person accused of writing the letter agreed that it was his letter, but an addition had been made to the letter that was not in his handwriting. The letter was written in blue ballpoint pen on lined notebook paper. The source of the threatening language in the questioned letter was written in one short sentence between two paragraphs. Striation patterns in ballpoint pens can develop and may be used to distinguish similar pens. Striations are caused by debris or defects on the housing of the pen tip, which holds the ball in place (Lewis, 2003). In this case, the questioned sentence written with blue ballpoint pen had different striation patterns than the rest of

FIGURE 7.11 A blue ballpoint pen with a complex striation pattern used courtesy of Dr. Valery Aginsky.

the blue ballpoint pen writing on the document. This evidence supported the contention that the questioned sentence was written with a different pen from the writing on the rest of the body of the letter. Distinct striation patterns occurred in examples from two different ballpoint pens. Striation patterns may help differentiate one pen from another. Unlike the case example described above, one pen is blue ink and the other is black ink. These two pens are good examples of two types of striation patterns. Figure 7.11 is a complex striation pattern written with a blue ballpoint pen. Figure 7.12 is a simple striation pattern with a large non-inked area of skipping in the ink line.

Check Alterations

Foster and Freeman issued a sample altered check to be used as a quality control standard for the Video Spectral Comparator-1 (VSC-1) in the late 1990s. The check was

FIGURE 7.12 A black ballpoint pen with a simple striation pattern and an area of skipping in the ink line used courtesy of Dr. Valery Aginsky.

written with one black ballpoint pen ink pen and altered with a visually similar but different black ballpoint pen. The image in Figure 7.13 shows two portions of a sample altered check viewed with the VSC-1. Alterations luminesced or glowed when excited with blue-green light and viewed through a camera sensitive to reactions in the infrared part of the electromagnetic spectrum. The original writing absorbed or darkened.

Simulated Signature Case

The signature on a contract was in question. The contract was dated July 30, 2013. A known writing sample contemporaneous with the questioned contract was submitted. The questioned signature was slowly written with heavy pressure, and blunt beginning and ending strokes. The known writing sample showed a high level of skill and fluency of the line quality. The

FIGURE 7.13 Two portions of a sample altered check viewed with the VSC-1. Alterations luminesced when excited with blue-green light and viewed through a camera sensitive to reactions in the infrared part of the spectrum. The original writing absorbed or darkened.

differences between the line quality and fluency of the questioned signature compared with the known signatures supported the contention that the questioned signature was a simulation rather than a genuine signature. Figure 7.14 is a chart comparing the questioned and known signatures in this case.

Conclusion

These cases represent typical simple cases received by FDEs in government laboratories and private

FIGURE 7.14 Simulated signature chart showing the questioned signature above and known signatures for comparison below.

practice. These cases included charts with images of the questioned and known writings, or simply questioned writings to demonstrate the findings. Disputed handwriting formed the central questioned material in most of the cases. Forensic document examination includes more than just handwriting, but the majority of the casework involves disputed handwriting.

References

Lewis, J., 2003. Striation patterns in new and used ballpoint pens. J. Am. Soc. Questioned Document Exam. 2 (6), 67–71.

Lewis, J., June 4–5, 2013. Current bank check scanning practices. Presentation at the Measurement Science & Standards in Forensic Handwriting Analysis conference sponsored by the National Institute of Standards & Technology in Gaithersburg, Maryland.

Masson, J., 2012. Scanned images: how well do they depict the subtle features in handwriting? J. Am. Soc. Questioned Document Exam 15 (1), 41–47.

CHAPTER 8

Standards for Forensic Document Examiners

Chapter Outline

Forensic Document Examination. http://dx.doi.org/10.1016/B978-0-12-416693-6.00008-4

Excellence costs a great deal.
(May Sarton, The Small Room, 1961)

Introduction

Forensic document examiners (FDEs) follow standards for methodology and competence. An array of 21 standards developed by the Scientific Working Group for Forensic Document Examination (SWGDOC) was published by ASTM International covering the Scope of Work of Forensic Document Examiners to a Standard for Altered Documents and many more specific examinations. Beginning in 2012, the ASTM standards pertaining to FDE began to be replaced as they expire by standards generated by SWGDOC. The American Board of Forensic Document Examiners (ABFDE) continues to certify the competence of FDEs through their testing and certification program.

Standardization in Questioned Document Literature

Before ASTM and SWGDOC standards became ubiquitous and vital to FDEs, several questioned document authors discussed standards in a more general way in their books.

Roy Huber offered standards for FDEs for the examination of handwriting. His suggested standards included sections with the following titles: "The Protection of Material," "The Approach to Examination and Study," "The Basis of Reporting Results," "The Certainty of Conclusions," and "The Assertion of Qualifications" (Huber and Headrick, 1999).

David Ellen discussed quality assurance in his book (Ellen, 2006). He mentioned the importance of reliable methods and the importance of competence of FDEs (ibid). Outside testing of the competence of FDEs by researchers like Dr. Kam (Kam et al., 1994) was cited as an example of quality assurance in the profession (Ellen, 2006).

Kirsten Jackson and Jan Seaman Kelly wrote directly about ASTM standards related to FDE in a chapter titled "Preparation for a Daubert Hearing" in the fine book *Scientific Examination of Questioned Documents, Second Edition*, edited by Jan Seaman Kelly and Brian Lindblom (Kelly and Lindblom, 2006). Since the *Daubert v. Merrill Dow Pharmaceuticals, Inc.*, U.S. Supreme Court 509 U.S. 579, (Daubert, 1993) decision the reliability of a scientific discipline must satisfy five criteria. These criteria, known as the Daubert factors, include:

1. General acceptance.

2. Whether the theory or technique has been tested.

3. Whether the technique has been subject to peer review and publication.

4. The existence and maintenance of standards controlling the technique's operation.

5. The known or potential error rate.

The Daubert decision intended to ease the admittance of new scientific evidence in court, but the five Daubert factors were actually used to attack and disqualify established forensic experts. These factors were meant to serve as guides for judges to assess scientific methods, and each factor did not have to be met. The approach of FDEs has been to address how our discipline meets each factor.

Kelly and Jackson (2006) listed ASTM published standards related to FDE as guidelines that fulfilled the fourth Daubert factor, which calls for proving the existence and maintenance of standards controlling the technique's operation. This chapter lists the ASTM standards pertaining to FDE at the time of publication.

ASTM International Standards

ASTM International, previously called the American Society for Testing and Materials (ASTM), is an international developer of voluntary consensus standards for industry and forensic sciences. ASTM originated in 1898 (ASTM, 2013). The founders were engineers and chemists at the Pennsylvania Railroad. ASTM International serves a wide group of industries through 144 standard-writing committees (ibid). ASTM International's headquarters is in West Conshohocken, Pennsylvania (ibid).

In 1970 the ASTM Committee E30 on Forensic Science originated, and soon after in 1972 published its first standard E444 Guide for Scope of the Work of Forensic Document Examiners (Vargas, 2008). The ASTM E30 Committee included six subcommittees, with E30.02 on Questioned Documents gaining more than 200 members and 20 standards approved by the group (ibid) (SWGDOC, 2013).

SWGDOC

The Scientific Working Group for Questioned Documents (SWGDOC) evolved from the Technical Working Group for Questioned Documents which began in 1997 (Riordan et al., 2013). The group includes FDEs from federal, state, and county laboratories and private practitioners. They meet at the FBI Academy in Quantico, Virginia (ibid).

SWGDOC developed drafts and updates of standards for FDEs and originally published them through ASTM International. Since 2012, SWGDOC has published standards that they developed on their website rather than through ASTM International. The standards are readily available and free to all on the SWGDOC website (SWGDOC, 2013). The mission of SWGDOC is to gather together FDEs in order to:

- *Define the scope and practice areas of the profession.*
- *Standardize operating procedures, protocols, and terminology.*
- *Consolidate and enhance the profession of forensic document examination.*
- *Promote self-regulation, documentation, training, continuing education, and research (ibid).*

The goals of SWGDOC published on their website include:

- *Strengthen the content and the enforcement of published performance standards.*
- *Continue to write and foster the publication of performance standards for sub-discipline examinations.*
- *Publish and maintain the Daubert Factors for Attorneys and Daubert Factors for Forensic Document Examiners presentations (as they relate to forensic document examination).*
- *Participate in and support a Human Factors Working Group for Forensic Document Examination.*
- *Expand the participant pool to include academicians, statisticians, legal professionals, and practitioners from other forensic disciplines (ibid).*

SWGDOC has available 21 peer-reviewed published standards. They are the product of public and private FDEs along with academic researchers (ibid). The 21 SWGDOC Standards published to date are the following:

SWGDOC Standard for Scope of Work of Forensic Document Examiners

SWGDOC Standard for Test Methods for Forensic Writing Ink Comparison

SWGDOC Terminology for Expressing Conclusions of Forensic Document Examiners

SWGDOC Standard for Writing Ink Identification

SWGDOC Terminology Relating to the Examination of Questioned Documents

SWGDOC Standard for Examination of Mechanical Checkwriter Impressions

SWGDOC Standard for Examination of Dry Seal Impressions

SWGDOC Standard for Examination of Fracture Patterns and Paper Fiber Impressions on Single-Strike Film Ribbons and Typed Text

SWGDOC Standard for Physical Match of Paper Cuts, Tears, and Perforations in Forensic Document Examinations

SWGDOC Standard for Examination of Rubber Stamp Impressions

SWGDOC Standard for Examination of Handwritten Items

SWGDOC Standard for Indentation Examinations

SWGDOC Standard for Non-destructive Examination of Paper

SWGDOC Standard for Examination of Altered Documents

SWGDOC Standard for Minimum Training Requirements for Forensic Document Examiners

SWGDOC Standard for Examination of Documents Produced with Liquid Ink Jet Technology

SWGDOC Standard for Examination of Documents Produced with Toner Technology

SWGDOC Standard for Examination of Typewritten Items

SWGDOC Standard for Preservation of Charred Documents

SWGDOC Standard for Preservation of Liquid Soaked Documents

SWGDOC Standard for Use of Image Capture and Storage Technology in Forensic Document Examination (ibid)

American Board of Forensic Document Examiners (ABFDE) Certification

The American Board of Forensic Document Examiners (ABFDE) was formed in Washington, D.C. in 1977. An LEAA grant from the Forensic Science Foundation helped found the ABFDE (Riordan et al., 2013). In 2013, 111 FDEs hold certification from ABFDE (ABFDE, 2013). The Board describes its purpose and sponsorship this way:

> *The Board's objectives are two-fold: to establish, maintain and enhance standards of qualification for those who practice forensic document examination, and to certify applicants who comply with ABFDE requirements for this expertise. In doing so, the Board aims to safeguard the public interest by ensuring that anyone who claims to be a specialist in forensic document examination does, in fact, possess the necessary skills and qualifications. The ABFDE is sponsored by the* **Canadian Society of Forensic Science**, *the* **American Society of Questioned Document Examiners**, *the* **Southwestern Association of Forensic Document Examiners**, *and the* **Southeastern Association of Forensic Document Examiners**, *and also is recognized by the* **American Academy of Forensic Sciences**, *the* **International**

> **Association for Identification**, *the* **Midwestern Association of Forensic Scientists**, *and the* **Mid-Atlantic Association of Forensic Scientists.** *The ABFDE is the only certifying body that can claim such sponsorship and recognition.*

A candidate for certification must be a resident of the United States of America, Canada, Australia, or New Zealand. At minimum, a baccalaureate degree from an accredited college is required. Professional experience must include a fulltime, two-year training program in a laboratory recognized by the Board. The training program must meet basic requirements of the SWG-DOC Standard for Minimum Training Requirements for Forensic Document Examiners. A testing program including written and practical problems and an oral board examination must be successfully completed. Recertification is required every five years (ibid).

ABFDE-certified examiners work at all of the major federal laboratories, including: the Federal Bureau of Investigation (FBI), the U.S. Secret Service, the Internal Revenue Service, U.S. Immigration and Customs Enforcement, the U.S. Postal Inspection Service, the Bureau of Alcohol, Tobacco and Firearms (ATF), the U.S. Army Criminal Investigation Crime Laboratory, and the Department of Veterans Affairs. ABFDE-certified examiners also work at state and county laboratories and in private practice.

In federal and state job announcements, qualification requirements often list certification by ABFDE as a required or desired accomplishment for applicants.

References

ABFDE, The American Board of Forensic Document Examiners. <http://www.abfde.org/> (accessed 10.14.13).

ASTM International. <http://www.astm.org/ABOUT/overview.html> (accessed 10.14.13).

Daubert v. Merrell Dow Pharmaceuticals Inc., 113 S. Ct. 2786 (1993).

Ellen, D., 2006. Scientific Examination of Documents: Methods and Techniques, third ed. CRC Press, Taylor & Francis Group, Boca Raton, Florida.

Huber, R.A., Headrick, A.M., 1999. Handwriting Identification Facts and Fundamentals. CRC Press, Taylor & Francis Group, Boca Raton, Florida.

Kam, M., Wetstein, J., Conn, R., 1994. Proficiency of professional document examiners in writer identification, Journal of Forensic Sciences, 39, 5.

Kelly, J.S., Jackson, K., 2006. "Preparation for a Daubert Hearing." In: Kelly, J.S., Lindblom, B. (Eds.), Scientific Examination of Questioned Documents, Second Edition. CRC Press, Taylor & Francis Group, Boca Raton, Florida, pp. 385–392.

Kelly, J.S., Lindblom, B., Eds., 2006. Scientific Examination of Questioned Documents, Second Edition. CRC Press, Taylor & Francis Group, Boca Raton, Florida.

Riordan, W.M., Gustafson, J.A., Fitzgerald, M.P., Lewis, J.A., 2013. Forensic document examination. In: Ubelaker, D.H. (Ed.), Forensic Science: Current Issues, Future Directions. Wiley-Blackwell, Chichester, West Sussex, UK, pp. 224–251.

SWGDOC, The Scientific Working Group for Questioned Documents. <http://www.swgdoc.org> (accessed 14.10.13).

Vargas, R., 2008. Standards for Questioned Document Examination. ASTM International Standardization News, November/December. <http://www.astm.org/SNEWS/ND_2008/vargas_nd08.html> (accessed 10.14.13).

CHAPTER 9

Forensic Document Examination in the Courts

Chapter Outline

Forensic Document Examination. http://dx.doi.org/10.1016/B978-0-12-416693-6.00009-6

Fairness is what justice really is.
(Potter Stewart, Time, October 20, 1958)

Before 1900

Forgery evolved along with the development of handwriting. Testimony for forensic document examiners began in the English-speaking courts with the case of *Goodtitle d. Revett v. Braham* in 1792 (Huber and Headrick, 1999). Two experts qualified to testify based on their experience as inspectors of franks (ibid). Expert testimony in questioned documents was admitted in Massachusetts in 1836 in the case *Moody v. Rowell* (ibid).

Early questioned document cases in the United States were hampered by limiting known writings in a case to only those already in evidence following the English common law practice. Court decisions in Massachusetts in 1814, followed later by Connecticut and Vermont, allowed the submission of other known writing samples (Hilton, 1979). This expansion of known writings available for submission in a case improved the quality of handwriting comparisons.

In the late 1800s, forensic document examination was expanded to include testimony on inks and typewriting (Levinson, 2001). Books published by early forensic document examiners included: *A Treatise on Disputed Handwriting* (1894) by William Elijah Hagan, *Manual for the Study of Documents* (1894) by Persifor Frazer, and *Ames on Forgery* (1899, 1901) by Daniel T. Ames (Riordan et al., 2013).

The 20th-Century Courts

Albert S. Osborn, with his book *Questioned Documents* in 1910, is considered the father of questioned documents (Osborn, 1910). He expanded the work beyond handwriting to include paper examinations, and ink and typewriter examinations (Huber and Headrick, 1999). Osborn's pioneering work in forensic document examination through his testimonies, lectures, and books helped broaden the use of forensic document examination in the courts. For more about Albert S. Osborn see Chapter 2.

United States courts have relied on forensic document examiner (FDE) testimony for more than a century. In 1913, a U.S. statute allowed known writings to be admitted in court for comparison with questioned writing (Vargas, 2008). The Frye rule, based on the *Frye v. U.S.*, 293 F1013 (D.C. Cir. 1923) case, required that expert testimony must have gained general acceptance in the particular discipline in order to be admitted (ibid).

In 1975, the Federal Rules of Evidence gave courts broader power to decide on expert witness admissibility (ibid). The Frye and Federal Rules of Evidence were in place until 1993. The United States Supreme Court ruled in *Daubert v. Merrell Dow Pharmaceuticals*, 509 U.S. 579 (1993), that additional factors may be considered for the admission of scientific evidence. The Frye standard of general acceptance was incorporated as one of the flexible Daubert factors.

The Daubert factors set out to determine the reliability of scientific evidence by asking:

1. whether the theory could be tested,

2. whether there were standards,

3. whether there were publications in peer-reviewed literature,

4. whether there was general acceptance in the particular discipline, and

5. whether a known error rate could be developed.

The Daubert decision sought to expand the admission of novel scientific evidence. It was not intended to apply to well-established forensic science disciplines like forensic document examination. Forensic document examination was not new; FDE testimony has been part of solid case preparation in the United States courts for more than 100 years. It was also not novel; the Questioned Document Section was one of the founding sections of the American Academy of Forensic Sciences in 1948.

Following the Daubert decision, the judge ruled in *U.S. v. Starzecpyzel*, 880 F. Suppl. 1027 (S.D.N.Y., 1995) that Daubert did not apply to forensic document examination because it did not meet the Daubert criteria, but was still admissible as a technical skill. This case caused FDEs to carefully review empirical studies in the field and to begin publishing more research to prove the individuality of handwriting. Courts had never before required FDEs to prove through empirical studies that handwriting was individual or that FDEs are more proficient in identifying handwriting than the layman. Those days of general acceptance were gone and a golden age of research for FDEs was initiated.

Following Daubert, in *General Electric v. Joiner*, 78 F.3d 524 (1997), a judge was given greater leeway to reject opinion testimony, and in *Kumho Tire v. Carmichael*, 526 U.S. 137, 119 S. Ct. 1167, 143 L.Ed.2d 238 (1999), the Daubert factors were extended to include scientific as well as technical or other specialized expert opinion testimony (Riordan et al., 2013).

The Critics

In 1989 a law review article titled *Exorcism of Ignorance as a Proxy for Rational Knowledge: The Lessons of Handwriting Identification Expertise* (Risinger et al., 1989) attacked forensic document examination and compared FDE to witchcraft. Forensic document examiners dismissed the article completely because it was filled with inaccuracies, was not a peer-reviewed publication, and the three authors were not trained in forensic document examination. The arguments that the authors made against FDEs resurfaced after the Daubert decision. In fact, the authors made a cottage industry out of opposing FDEs in court as expert critics. Responses to the critics appear in research on the admissibility of handwriting evidence in court published by Vastrick (Vastrik, 2004) and by Moenssens in his law review article *Handwriting Identification Evidence in the Post-Daubert World* (Moenssens, 1997).

The American Board of Forensic Document Examiners

Challenges to FDEs in court were met by the American Board of Forensic Document Examiners (ABFDE). The Daubert Group consisting of three FDEs was formed within ABFDE to help track Daubert hearings involving FDEs around the country, and to provide a concise guide to show how FDEs meet each of the Daubert factors for the admission of scientific opinion testimony (Riordan et al., 2013). The Daubert Group has assisted FDEs successfully in more than 30 Daubert hearings (ibid).

Forensic Document Examiners Meet Each Daubert Factor

The basic theory in forensic document examination regarding handwriting is that no two people write exactly alike. The individuality of handwriting has been successfully proven through consideration of the five Daubert factors. The following material, which explains how forensic handwriting identification meets each Daubert factor, is based on a PowerPoint presentation developed by Kirsten Singer and Jan Seaman Kelly (Singer and Kelly, 2012).

1. Theory Tested

The individuality of handwriting has been validated through computer-based research programs including: CEDARFOX, developed by Dr. Sargur Srihari et al. at the State University of New York, Buffalo; FLASH ID, developed by Gannon Technologies Group in Alexandria, Virginia; and FISH, developed by the BKA in Germany and the U.S. Secret Service.

In an article titled "Individuality of Handwriting" in the *Journal of Forensic Sciences,* Dr. Sargur N. Srihari presented research that found that based on the consideration of only eight characteristics, the computer system identified each of the 1,500 writers in the study with a 98% confidence level. When considering more than eight characteristics, the research suggested that the confidence level would approach 100% (Srihari, 2002).

FLASH ID (Forensic Language-Independent Analysis System for Handwriting Identification) is a software program that uses handwriting to identify writers. Handwriting is scanned into a database, and biometric content is extracted and saved as image files. FLASH ID converts images of handwriting into graphemes. Graphemes may consist of portions of letters, whole letters, or groups of letters. Graphemes are classified by their topology and geometric features. Statistical analysis of the topology and geometric features of the graphemes helps to distinguish one writer from another. A profile is established for each handwriting sample and compared to other profiles in the FLASH ID Database Builder (Walch and Gantz, 2013). FLASH ID is not in general use to date outside of a few large government laboratories.

FISH (Forensic Information System for Handwriting) is a database used by large government laboratories in the United States and Germany. FISH is based on the individuality of handwriting. In the United States Secret Service laboratory database and international databases, out of more than 110,000 writers, no two have demonstrated exactly the same handwriting characteristics (Dusak, 1993; Singer and Kelly, 2012).

Twins write more similarly than non-twins, but their handwritings can be discriminated by FDEs and computer examination programs, further supporting the theory of the individuality of handwriting. The study *On the Discriminability of the Handwriting of Twins* (Srihari et al., 2008) found that in comparing verification samples of non-twins and pairs of twins, there was an 87% correct verification rate result for twins, and a 96% correct verification rate for non-twins. Laypersons performed poorer than the computer, but forensic document examiners outperformed the computer.

Other twins handwriting research that supports the theory of the individuality of handwriting includes: *An Investigation into the Degree of Similarity in the Handwriting of Identical and Fraternal Twins in New Zealand* (Boot, 1998), *The Handwriting of Identical Twins* (Gamble, 1980), and *A Statistical Study of Handwritings by Twins and Other Persons of Multiple Births* (Beacom, 1960).

Additional general research that supports the theory of the individuality of handwriting includes: *The Determination of Authorship from a Homogenous Group of Writers* (Durina and Caligiuri, 2009), *Lineup: The Reliability of Examinations Involving Multiple Writers* (Parrett and Szabo, 2003), *A Study of the Occurrence of Certain Characteristics in a Random Population* (Horton, 1996), *Case Report: The Individuality of Handwriting Demonstrated Through the Field Screening of 1000 Writers* (Shiver, 1996), *A Review of Handwriting Search Cases as an Indicator of the Individuality of Handwriting* (Welch, 1999), *The Uniqueness of Writing* (Huber, 1990), *The Large Scale Searching of Handwriting Samples* (Baxendale and Renshaw, 1979), and *A Statistical Examination of Selected Handwriting Characteristics* (Muehlberger, 1977).

2. Standards

SWGDOC (The Scientific Working Group for Forensic Document Examination) has published 21 standards for FDEs to date. Standards for FDEs published by SWGDOC and ASTM, and certification by the American Board of Forensic Document Examiners (ABFDE) are all discussed in detail in Chapter 8.

3. Peer Review and Publications

Forensic document examination research is published in many peer-reviewed journals, including:

- Journal of Forensic Sciences
- Journal of the American Society of Questioned Document Examiners
- International Journal of Forensic Document Examiners
- Canadian Society of Forensic Science Journal
- Journal of Forensic Identification
- Forensic Science International
- Journal of Police Science and Administration
- Journal of the Forensic Science Society
- Journal of Criminal Law and Criminology

Research papers on forensic document examination are presented at the annual scientific sessions of the following forensic science organizations:

- American Academy of Forensic Sciences
- American Society of Questioned Document Examiners
- International Association of Forensic Sciences
- International Association for Identification

- Mid-Atlantic Association of Forensic Scientists
- Midwestern Association of Forensic Scientists
- Northeastern Association of Forensic Scientists
- Southeastern Association of Forensic Document Examiners
- Southwestern Association of Forensic Document Examiners

SWGDOC standards are peer reviewed by the forensic document community before publication, which also helps to satisfy the peer review and publications factor of Daubert.

4. General Acceptance

The expertise of FDEs has been accepted in United States courts for more than 100 years (*Suave v. Dawson*, LA, 1812). Every major law enforcement organization offers FDE expertise. The validity of FDE is supported by all scientific reference material. Federal appellate court decisions all have concluded that forensic document examination fulfills the Daubert factors.

Questioned document sections are part of the following multidiscipline forensic science organizations:

- American Academy of Forensic Sciences
- International Association for Identification

- Canadian Society of Forensic Science
- British Academy of Forensic Sciences Society
- Australian and New Zealand Forensic Science Society
- European Network of Forensic Science Institutes
- International Association of Forensic Sciences

The theory of forensic handwriting identification has been proven valid in court through judicial notice, statutory recognition, stipulation and evidentiary tests, and cross-examination.

Courses in forensic document examination are included in graduate degrees and baccalaureate forensic science degrees at the following universities:

- The George Washington University
- Michigan State University
- John Jay College
- National University (San Diego)
- University of Alabama at Birmingham
- University of New Haven

- University of Central Oklahoma
- University of Illinois at Chicago

5. Error Rate

Forensic document examination, like many other forensic science disciplines, does not have an error rate. It is not possible to calculate because each case's evidence and every examiner examining the evidence is unique. The examinations in one case will vary considerably from the examinations required in another case. Research testing the proficiency of FDEs confirms that the skill of FDEs exists, and FDEs perform better than laymen in identifying and eliminating the writers of questioned documents. In the following articles, research by Dr. Moshe Kam supports the proficiency of FDEs:

1. *Proficiency of Professional Document Examiners in Writer Identification* (Kam et al., 1994). In this study, FDEs performed better than college graduates who were non-experts.

2. *Writer Identification by Professional Document Examiners* (Kam et al., 1997). Laymen were six times more likely than FDEs to incorrectly identify questioned writing.

3. *Signature Authentication by Forensic Document Examiners* (Kam et al., 2001). In this study, FDEs had a 0.49% error rate compared to a 6.47% error rate for laymen.

4. *Writer Identification Using Hand Printed and Non-Hand Printed Questioned Documents* (Kam and Lin, 2003). Laymen incorrectly identified hand printed documents at a 40.45% rate, while FDEs incorrectly identified hand printing at a 9.3% rate.

Research from Sita, Found, and Rogers titled *Forensic Handwriting Examiners' Expertise for Signature Comparison* (Sita et al., 2002) found the error rates for FDEs resulted in 3.4% (uncalled) and 5.8% (called). Laymen error rates measured 19.3% (uncalled) and 25.3% (called).

Research by Dr. Kam and Dr. Found proved that FDEs performed significantly better than laymen. Expert opinions from FDEs helps prevent incorrect conclusions from laymen in questioned document cases.

Early Court Challenges

In the case *U.S. v. Timothy James McVeigh* in 1997, an attempt was made to limit the testimony of an FDE in the case. The court decided that the FDE would be limited to demonstrating similarities and differences, but could not express an opinion. The witness was not called by the prosecution. This case started more Daubert challenges to cases involving FDEs (Vargas, 2008). In *U.S. v. Kent Rutherford* in 2000, the FDE was limited to demonstrating similarities and differences in the case, but could not express an opinion. Soon after the case *U.S. v. Chan Ian Saelee* in 2001, the FDE was excluded from testifying (ibid).

21st-Century Courts

Forensic document examiners (FDEs) began to increase production of basic research in response to a few early Daubert exclusions. They also organized existing research in support of the basic theory of the identification of handwriting for attorneys so that they would be prepared to counter Daubert challenges (ibid). The existing Scientific Working Group for Forensic Document Examination (SWGDOC) organized and standardized methodology, terminology, and training requirements for FDEs.

The following cases are from Federal Circuit Appellate Courts where Daubert motions to exclude forensic handwriting analysis testimony were denied (Singer, 2013):

1. **U.S. v. Jawara,** No. 05-30266 (9th Cir. Sept 2006).
2. **U.S. v. Tunde Adeyi,** No. 05-1722-cr (2nd Cir. 2006).
3. **U.S. v. Al James Smith**, 2005 U.S. App. LEXIS 23798 (4th Cir. 2005).
4. **U.S. v. Judson Brown**, 2005 U.S. App. LEXIS 22703 (2nd Cir. April 2003).
5. **U.S. v. Christopher Mornan,** No. 04-1319 (3rd Cir. 2005).
6. **U.S. v. Chris Rutland and Barbara Grams,** Crim. No. 02-494(DRD) (3rd Cir. 2004).

7. **U.S. v. Demanjuk**, 1:99 CV1193, U.S. District Court, Cleveland, Ohio (6th Cir. 2004).

8. **U.S. v. Prime**, 02-30375, D.C. No. CR-01-00310-RSL (9th Cir. 2004).

9. **U.S. v. Crisp,** 324 F.3d 261, 271 (4th Cir. 2003) (fingerprints and handwriting).

10. **U.S. v. Martha Elena Gonzales**, aka Marta Gonzales, 95-3261; **U.S. v. Jose Ramiro Valenzuela-Obeso,** aka Ramiro Valenzuela, 95-3263; **U.S. v. Juan Manuel Valenzuela-Obeso**, aka Kiki and aka Miti, 95-3370; **U.S. v. Patricia Camerina Lopez** (8th Cir. 2003).

11. **U.S. v. Dennis J. Mooney**, 315 F.3d 54, 520-63 (1st Cir. 2002).

12. **U.S. v. Hernandez,** 2002 U.S. App. LEXIS 12153; 89 A.F.T.R.2d (RIA) 3049 (10th Cir. 2002).

13. **U.S. v. Kehoe,** 310 F. 3d 579, 593 (8th Cir. 2002).

14. **U.S. v. Johnson**, 39 Fed, Appx. 685, 2002 WL 44242 (9th Cir. 2002) (unpublished op).

15. **U.S. v. Elmore**, 56 M.J. 533 (Navy-Marine Ct. App 2001).

16. **U.S. v. Jeremiah Bryant Och,** U.S. App. LEXIS 17077;16 Fed. Appx. 666, No. 00-10351 (9th Cir. 2001).

17. **U.S. v. Jolivet**, 224 F.3d 902, 905-06 (8th Cir. 2000).

18. **U.S. v. Battle**, 188 F.3d 519, 1999 WL 596966 (10th Cir. 1999) (unpublished).

19. **U.S. v. Paul,** 175 F.3d 906, 910-11 (11th Cir. 1999).

20. **U.S. v. Mohamed Ijaz Chohan,** U.S. App. LEXIS 17487, No. 97-1010 (2nd Cir. 1997).

21. **U.S. v. Jones,** 107 F.2d 1147, 1156-60 (6th Cir. 1997).

22. **U.S. v. Rosario,** 118 F.3d 160, 163-64 (3rd Cir. 1997).

23. **U.S. v. Ruth**, 46 M.J. 1 (Armed Forces Ct. App. 1997).

24. **U.S. v. Velasquez**, 64 F.3d 844, 848-50 (3rd Cir. 1995).

The following cases are from U.S. District Courts where Daubert motions to exclude forensic handwriting analysis testimony were denied (Singer, 2013):

1. **U.S. v. David H. Brooks and Sandra Hatfield**, EDNY No. 06-CR-550 (S-1)(JS) (2nd Cir. Jan 2010).

2. **United States of America v. Anthony Pendleton,** U.S. District Court, Los Angeles, California (9th Cir. Aug 2009).

3. **U.S. v. Robert Gaulden,** D.C. Superior Court 2008 CF2-20509.

4. **U.S. V. Isaac Yass and Robert A. Blechman**, No. 08040008-JAR. Hearing 11-10-08.

5. **U.S. v. Raymond Yono,** (Eastern District Michigan) Criminal Co. 06-CR-20479, Judge Patrick Duggan (June 2008, examiner Rich Dusak).

6. **U.S. v. Hanner,** HW, Pr Pro (3rd Cir. June 2007).

7. **U.S. v. Stephen Yagman** (9th Cir. May 2007).

8. **U.S. v. Weiss,** Criminal Case No. 05cr00179LTB (10th Cir. April 2007).

9. **U.S. v. David Lin,** Case No. CR 01-20071 RMW (9th Cir. Jan 2007).

10. **U.S. v. Juan Pena and Maria D. Pena** (5th Cir. Aug 2006).

11. **U.S. v. William C. Campbell**, Civil Action No. 1:04-CV-0424-RWS, 2006 U.S. Dist LEXIS 7442 (11th Cir. Feb 2006).

12. **U.S. v Ramon Fashola,** Crim No 1:04-CR-372-JEC, NDGA (11th Cir. Feb 2006).

13. **U.S. v. Ferguson,** Case No. 3:03cr019 (6th Cir. Aug 2004).

14. **U.S. v. Pirchesky,** Case No. 01-608-CR-SEITZ (11th Cir. Aug 2004).

15. **U.S. v. Jeffrey H. Feingold,** CR 02-0976-PHX-SMM (9th Cir. April 2004).

16. **U.S. v. Shawn Joshua Johnson** (5th Cir. April 2004).

17. **U.S. v. William E. Lecroy, Jr.**, Criminal Indictment No. 2:02-CR-038) (11th Cir. Jan 2004).

18. **U.S. v. Bobby R. Smart** (11th Cir. Sept 2003).

19. **U.S. v. Jose de Jesus Garcia-Flores**, et al. (5th Cir. Aug 2003).

20. **U.S. v. Henry Xie**, California, CR 03-00137 CRB (9th Cir. 2003).

21. **U.S. v. Jack Robert Urich**, CR-S-02-454-RLH (LRL) (9th Cir. 2003).

22. **United States v. Sanders**, No. 01-2646 (6th Cir. March 2003) (unpublished).

23. **U.S. v. Roberto Morejon**, Case No. 99-717-CR-Seitz (11th Cir. July 2003).

24. **U.S. v. Janet Thornton**, Wichita, Kansas (10th Cir. Jan 2003).

25. **U.S. v. Chris Rutland and Barbara Grams**, Feb 2003, Crim. No. 02-494(DRD), District of New Jersey, Judge Debevoise.

26. **U.S. v Judson Brown**, 3:02CR302(JCH) (2nd Cir. April 2003).

27. **U.S. v. Giorgies**, 29 Fed. Appx. 472, 2002 WL 89728 (9th Cir. 2002) (unpublished).

28. **U.S. v. Gricco**, 2002 WL 746037 (3rd Cir. 2002).

29. **U.S. v. Broten**, NY, Case No. 01-CR-411 (DNH) (2nd Cir. 2002).

30. **U.S. v. Frank M. Patti, Sr. and Alice G. Guy**, Judge Lacey Collier (based in part on **U.S. v. Paul**) (11th Cir. 2002).

31. **U.S. v. Lindsey**, U.S. District CR No. 00-00482DAE (9th Cir. 2002).

32. **U.S. v. Laphonse Akilo Young**, Criminal No. 02-0075-CB (11th Cir. 2002).

33. **U.S. v. Ramos**, EDNY 01 CR 0015 (ARR), Sept 2002.

34. **U.S. v. Michael Prime**, 220 F. Supp. 2d 1203 (W.D Wash. 2002) (9th Cir. 2002).

35. **Commodity Futures Trading Commission and Timothy D. Moratzka v. Leonard G. Nauman**, U.S. Bankruptcy Court, District of Minnesota, BKY No. 00-45285-NCD ADV. NO. 01-4272-NCD (8th Cir. 2002).

36. **U.S. v. Terry Kirby**, 1:01-CR-642, U.S. District Court, Georgia (11th Cir. 2001).

37. **U.S. v. Kenneth Richmond**, WL 1117735, LA (5th Cir. 2001).

38. **U.S. v. Steger**, Phoenix, Arizona (9th Cir. 2001).

39. **U.S. v. Och**, 16 Fed. Appx. 666, 2001 WL 867892 (9th Cir. 2001) (unpublished).

40. **U.S. v. Brenda K. Johnson**, Alexandria, Virgina (4th Cir. 2001).

41. **U.S. v. Demanjuk**, 1:99CV1193, U.S. District Court, Cleveland, Ohio. The judge indicated in his ruling complete trust in the document examinations that were conducted and indicated the ruling was in large part as a result of the document examiner's findings (May 2001).

42. **U.S. v. Pham**, #CR99-297 (9th Cir. 2000).

43. **U.S. v. Gilreath**, U.S. District Court, NDGA, No. 1:96-CR-472 JTC, Dec 1997.

44. **U.S. v. Reginald Keith Humphery**, No. 1:94-CR-447-JEC (11th Cir. 1997).

45. **U.S. v. Starzecpyzel**, 880 F.Supp 1027 (S.D.N.Y. 1995).

Daubert motions that resulted in limiting forensic handwriting analysis testimony (Singer, 2013):

1. **Legacy Vision, LLC v. Gary Yeamans,** CIV-04-1320-M, WD OK (10th Cir. June 2005).

2. **U.S. v. Yb-Lem Oskowitz**, 294 F. Supp. 2d 379, 384 (E.D.N.Y. 2003). In this case the FDE was not informed by the Assistant United States Attorney that a Daubert motion had been filed.

3. **Wolf v. Ramsey 1:00-CV-1187** (N.D. Ga. March 2003). The FDE was allowed to testify, but could not give an opinion (although there was no testimony because the judge granted summary judgment and dismissed the case).

4. **U.S. v. Hidalgo,** Phoenix, Arizona, U.S. Dist., CR-01-1011-PHX-FJM.

5. **U.S. v. Wanijiku Thiongo**, June 2002, Concord, New Hampshire.

6. **U.S. v. Kurtzke,** Jan 2002, Chicago, Illinois.

7. **U.S. v. Janeek Wiggan,** April 2000, Federal District Court, Southern District of West Virginia,

Charleston, West Virgina (4th Cir). Wiggan was charged with drug violations. The judge limited the testimony of the FDE without having a Daubert hearing.

8. **U.S. v. Rutherford,** 8:99CR120, U.S. Dist Ct (8th Cir. 2000).

9. **U.S. v. Hines**, Criminal No. 97-10336 NG, Massachusetts (1st Cir. 1999).

10. **U.S. v. Santillan,** WL 1201765 (N.D. Cal) (9th Cir. 1999).

Daubert motions that resulted in the complete exclusion of forensic handwriting analysis testimony (Singer, 2013):

1. **U.S. v. Fujii**, No. 00CR17, WL 33357453 (7th Cir. Sept 2000).

2. **U.S. v. Saelee**, No. A01-0084 CR (HRH) (9th Cir. 2001).

3. **U.S. v. Terry L. Brewer**, No. 01 CR 892, N.D. Illinois**,** 2002 U.S. Dist. LEXIS 6689, April 2002. The FDE was not present for the hearing and was unaware that a hearing took place. This decision was criticized by the judge in **U.S. v. Kirby**.

4. **U.S. v. Edward Lee Lewis**, Criminal Action No. 2:02-00042, in Southern District of West Virginia, Charleston, West Virginia, Aug 2002. The judge was the Honorable Joseph R. Goodwin.

5. **U.S. v. Plaza-Andrades** Utica, New York (2nd Cir. 2009). The FDE was not aware of or included in preparation for the motion *in limine* to exclude the testimony.

Miscellaneous cases involving Daubert challenges and the exclusion of professional critics (Singer, 2113):

1. **State v. Hull,** 10-29-08 Frye-Mack hearing, Minneapolis, Minnesota. The FDE was permitted to testify and the expert critic was not.

2. **U.S. v. Robert Pettus**, Criminal Case No. 2004 FEL 5721, Judge Neal Kravitz, Daubert hearing March 25, 2008 – April 2, 2008. (Superior Court of the District of Columbia Criminal Division – Felony Branch.) An FDE testified as an expert, and an expert critic also testified in the case.

3. **State v. Krueth,** 4-21-06 Anoka County Minnesota, Handwriting. Court asked for a Frye Mack hearing for an FDE. The FDE was allowed to testify and render opinion.

4. **U.S. v. Nowlin**, Sept 27, 2001, Appeal from Superior Court of the District of Columbia. This case is noteworthy in that the Federal Appellate Court for the District of Columbia, in their reversal, chastised the government for not having an FDE (handwriting expert) examine the writings and testify.

5. **Gebrendrias v. Ashcroft**, U.S. App. LEXIS 21013, No. 02-4254 (7th Cir. 2003) (unpublished). The 7th

Circuit Court of Appeals found that Daubert does not apply to immigration hearings. Gebrendrias, an Ethiopian woman seeking asylum, had challenged the testimony of the FDE. The challenge failed and admissibility of the evidence was affirmed.

6. **Progressive Business Systems et al. v. Superior Federal Bank**, Crawford County Circuit No. CIV 2000-30, June 24–25, 2004. This was a civil case that had to do with the examination of signatures on copies of checks. The expert critic was excluded from the trial.

7. **State of Nevada v. Warren, Tracy Morrell**, (2004) County No. 02F15712X, Metro No. 020828-0764. In this Daubert hearing, the FDE's testimony was admitted and the expert critic was excluded from the trial.

A Daubert motion in an electronic signature case:

AFLAC v. Biles, 2011, the United States District Court in the Southern District of Mississippi in a civil case, Civil Action No. 3:10CV667TSL-FKB, determined that an electronic signature created on a signature pad for a life insurance (American Family Life and Casualty – AFLAC) form was properly examined by importing the RAW signature data files and plotting the signature. An examination of a copy of the electronic signature on a form did not contain the same level of detail found in the electronic signature files.

Conclusion

Forensic document examiners, through more than a century of court testimony, have helped reveal the truth in disputed writing cases. Research supports the individuality of handwriting and the proficiency of FDEs. Each Daubert factor for the admission of scientific evidence is satisfied in forensic document examination. Daubert hearings continue to affirm new methods like the examination of disputed electronic signature files.

References

Baxendale, D., Renshaw, I.D., 1979. The large scale searching of handwriting samples. J. Forensic Sci. Soc. 19, 245.

Beacom, M., 1960. A study of handwriting by twins and other persons of multiple births. J. Forensic Sci. 5, 121–131.

Boot, D., 1998. An investigation into the degree of similarity in the handwriting of identical and fraternal twins in New Zealand. J. Am. Soc. Questioned Document Exam. 1 (2), 70–81.

Durina, M., Caligiuri, M.P., 2009. The determination of authorship from a homogenous group of writers. J. Am. Soc. Questioned Document Exam. 12, 77–90.

Dusak, R., February 15-20, 1993. The Forensic Information System for Handwriting: FISH A Laboratory Tool. Presentation at the Annual Meeting of the American Academy of Forensic Sciences in Boston, Massachusetts.

Gamble, D.J., 1980. The handwriting of identical twins. Canadian Soc. Forensic Sci. J. 13, 11–30.

Hilton, O., 1979. History of questioned document examination in the United States. J. Forensic Sci. 24 (4), 890–897.

Horton, R., 1996. A study of the occurrence of certain handwriting characteristics in a random population. Int. J. Forensic Document Exam. 2 (2), 95–102.

Huber, R., August, 1990. The uniqueness of writing. Presentation at the meeting of the American Society of Questioned Document Examiners in San Jose, California.

Huber, R., Headrick, A.M., 1999. Handwriting Identification: Facts and Fundamentals. CRC Press, Taylor & Francis Group, Boca Raton, Florida.

Kam, M., Lin, E., 2003. Writer identification using hand-printed and non-hand printed questioned documents. J. Forensic Sci. 48 (6), 1391–1395.

Kam, M., Fielding, G., Conn, R., 1997. Writer identification by professional document examiners. J. Forensic Sci. 42 (5), 778–786.

Kam, M., Wetstein, J., Conn, R., 1994. Proficiency of professional document examiners in writer identification. J. Forensic Sci. 39 (1), 5–14.

Kam, M., Gummadidala, K., Fielding, G., Conn, R., 2001. Signature authentication by forensic document examiners. J. Forensic Sci. 46 (4), 884–888.

Levinson, J., 2001. Questioned Documents, A Lawyer's Handbook. Academic Press, San Diego.

Moenssens, A., 1997. Handwriting identification evidence in the post-Daubert world. University of Missouri-Kansas City School of Law Law Review 66 (2), 252–343.

Muehlberger, R., Newman, K., Regent, J., Wichmann, J., 1977. A statistical examination of selected handwriting characteristics. J. Forensic Sci. 22, 206–215.

Osborn, A., 1910. Questioned Documents. Lawyers' Co-operative Publishing Co, Rochester, New York.

Parrett, D., Szabo, G., 2003. Lineup: the reliability of examinations involving multiple writers. J. Am. Soc. Questioned Document Exam. 6 (2), 82–84.

Riordan, W.M., Gustafson, J.A., Fitzgerald, M.P., Lewis, J.A., 2013. "Forensic document examination." In: Ubelaker, D.H. (Ed.), Forensic Science: Current Issues, Future Directions. Wiley-Blackwell, Chichester, West Sussex, UK, pp. 224–251.

Risinger, D., Denbeaux, M., Saks, M.J., 1989. Exorcism of ignorance as a proxy for rational knowledge: the lessons of handwriting identification expertise. University of Pennsylvania Law Review 137, 731–791.

Shiver, F., August, 1996. Case report: the individuality of handwriting demonstrated through the field screening of 1000 writers. Presentation at the American Society of Questioned Document Examiners annual meeting in Washington, D.C.

Singer, K., 2013. Forensic Document Examiner Veterans Administration personal contact, 7.25.13.

Singer, K., Seaman Kelly, J., 2012. PowerPoint presentation at http://www.swgdoc.org/index.php/resources.

Sita, J., Found, B., Rogers, D.K., 2002. Forensic handwriting examiner's expertise for signature comparison. J. Forensic Sci. 47 (5), 1117–1124.

Srihari, S., 2002. The individuality of handwriting. J. Forensic Sci. 47 (4), 856–872.

Srihari, S., Huang, C., Srinivasan, H., 2008. On the discriminability of the handwriting of twins. J. Forensic. Sci. 53 (2), 431–446.

Vargas, R. 2008. Standards for Questioned Document Examination. ASTM International Standardization News, November/December, www.astm.org/SNEWS/ND_2008/vargas_nd08.html (accessed 2013).

Vastrick, T., 2004. Admissibility issues in forensic document examination. J. Am. Soc. Questioned Document Exam. 7 (1), 37–47.

Walch, M., Gantz, D., June 4-5, 2013. The Forensic Language-Independent Analysis System for Handwriting Identification (FLASH ID). Presentation at the Measurement Science and Standards In Forensic Handwriting Analysis conference at The National Institute of Standards & Technology (NIST) in Gaithersburg, Maryland.

Welch, J.R., 1999. A review of handwriting search cases as an indicator of the individuality of handwriting: a test constructed to prove individuality in handwriting. Int. J. Forensic Document Examiners 5, 283–284.

CHAPTER 10

Court Preparation in Questioned Document Cases

Chapter Outline

Forensic Document Examination. http://dx.doi.org/10.1016/B978-0-12-416693-6.00010-2

Justice cannot be for one side alone, but must be for both…
(Eleanor Roosevelt, newspaper column, "My Day," October 15, 1947)

Introduction

Preparation for court begins when the case arrives for examination. Recording the date of submission eases the organization of the evidence later on in the case. An accurate description of the questioned and known documents received should appear in the case notes along with descriptions of all relevant tests and instrumentation used. Copies of all of the questioned and known items should be made. Charts supporting the basis for the findings in the case should accompany the case report.

Pretrial Conference

When an FDE receives a notification of a trial, hearing, or deposition date, he or she should book a pretrial conference with the attorney who submitted the case. This is not an optional activity. Lawyers may not wish to spend the time on a pretrial conference, but the FDE must insist. At minimum, a phone or Skype meeting must occur, but a face-to-face conference surpasses the effectiveness of either of these options. One of the most important tasks in the pretrial conference is conveying the FDE's qualification questions. Attorneys may assure the FDE that they excel at composing appropriate qualification questions for experts. This idea is fraught with peril. The FDE must be resolute on the use of familiar qualification questions. The expert knows best how to explain her education, training, and work experience. Here are some sample qualification questions:

1. Will you state your name?
2. What is your occupation?
3. How long have you been employed in the field of questioned documents?
4. Where do you work?
5. Are you certified?
6. What is your educational background?
7. What training have you received for the examination of questioned documents?
8. Have you received any additional training in the field of questioned documents?
9. Do you devote the majority of your time to the examination of questioned documents?
10. How are handwriting comparisons or examinations made?

11. Would you explain the basis for handwriting identification?

12. Are you a member of any professional organizations?

Attorney asks the court to accept the witness as an expert in the field of forensic document examination.

13. I hand you exhibit number ___, have you seen it before?

14. Have you examined it?

15. Who requested this examination?

16. For what purpose did you examine exhibit number ___?

17. As a result of your examination, do you have an opinion?

18. Do you have enlargements of these exhibits prepared to demonstrate your findings?

19. Are these true and accurate representations of exhibit number ___?

20. Will you produce these enlargements and identify them?

Attorney asks the court to mark the chart for demonstration.

21. Will you, with the aid of these enlargements, demonstrate your findings to the court and state your opinion?

Present an updated curriculum vitae to the attorney and discuss it. An explanation of the FDE's education, certification, and work experience prepares the attorney for questions from opposing counsel in court. Supply the attorney with copies of your recent publications and a list of the questioned document textbooks in your library. Inform your attorney of relevant literature concerning the particular examinations in this case. Discuss published standards created by the Scientific Working Group for Forensic Document Examination (SWG-DOC) that relate to the methods used in this case. Explain how forensic document examination meets the Daubert factors for admission of scientific evidence. See Chapter 9 for a detailed discussion of the Daubert factors and FDE. Define common questioned document terms like significant similarity, significant difference, and natural variation in handwriting for the attorney.

Ask these basic questions in the pretrial conference:

1. Where is the trial?

2. Who is the opposing attorney?

3. Who is the judge?

4. Is the court equipped with an ELMO (a projector for opaque items)?

5. Who is the opposing expert?

Tally the hours spent on the case and the total fees charged (for the FDE in private practice). Have your attorney introduce this information in court rather than waiting for the opposing counsel to do it.

Assess Credentials

Request the curriculum vitae of any opposing expert. Make a detailed study of the education, training, certification, and work experience listed. Assess whether the expert meets the minimum qualifications for certification by the American Board of Forensic Document Examiners (ABFDE). Those requirements include:

1. A baccalaureate degree.

2. Full-time training program in a recognized document laboratory.

3. Active practice of forensic document examination.

Sound-alike organizations that claim to have their own certification programs exist. Federal and state forensic science laboratories employ many FDEs across the

United States. Job announcements from these laboratories consistently list certification by ABFDE as a required or desired qualification for employment. If the opposing expert is self-trained, improperly trained, or is a graphologist, develop a line of questioning for your attorney to use. Graphology or graphonanalysis is the art of determining character traits from handwriting. Graphology is not forensic document examination. Graphologists who call themselves handwriting analysts are often confused with FDEs. The attorney should be made aware of the differences in training and methodologies between FDE and graphology. In *U.S. v. Bourgeois*, 950 F. 2d 980 (5th Cir. 1992), the testimony of a handwriting examiner was rejected, in part, because he completed his training in a correspondence school with an emphasis on graphology. It was also noted that the witness lacked certification from ABFDE.

Mainstream Forensic Science Organizations

Discuss the mainstream forensic science organizations with the attorney. Graphologists or poorly trained FDEs fail to meet the training and education requirements for these organizations. The mainstream forensic science organizations in the United States include:

1. The American Academy of Forensic Sciences (AAFS) Questioned Document Section

2. The American Society of Questioned Document Examiners (ASQDE)

3. The American Board of Forensic Document Examiners (ABFDE)

4. The Midwestern Association of Forensic Scientists (MAFS)

5. The Southwestern Association of Forensic Document Examiners (SWAFDE)

6. Mid-Atlantic Association of Forensic Scientists (MAAFS)

7. Southeastern Association of Forensic Document Examiners (SAFDE)

8. Northeastern Association of Forensic Scientists (NEAFS)

Other mainstream forensic science organizations include: the British Academy of Forensic Sciences Society, the Canadian Society of Forensic Science, The European Network of Forensic Science Institutes (ENFSI), the European Document Experts Working Group (EDEWG), and the European Network of Forensic Handwriting Experts (ENFHEX) (Riordan et al., 2013).

If the opposing expert is a graphologist, self-trained or poorly trained, and lists organizations on his or her curriculum vitae that are not mainstream forensic science organizations, have your attorney read the article *Expertise to Go* (Hansen, 2000).

Advise your attorney to establish through questioning of the opposing expert that his or her laboratory instrumentation includes items like: a stereo microscope, an electrostatic detection device (EDD) used to visualize latent indented writing on paper, a video spectral comparator (VSC) used to differentiate visually similar yet different inks, grids to detect misalignments and alterations to typewritten or computer-generated documents, and a flatbed scanner and digital or film camera to record images of questioned and known documents.

Court Charts

Discuss with the attorney the chart attached to your report. Determine what court exhibits best illustrate the case findings. If the courtroom offers little in the way of technology for projection of charts, use an enlarged chart on an easel or create enlarged handheld paper charts to publish to the attorneys, judge, and jury. Determine whether an ELMO which projects opaque items, is available. Charts made in a standard 8.5 × 11-inch paper size can be easily projected in the court with an ELMO. If the courtroom contains technology for computer projection of images, a PowerPoint presentation allows demonstration of the case findings. It is wise to have backup paper images of the PowerPoint demonstration in case of technical problems.

Direct and Cross-Examination

In pretrial, discuss information necessary to bring forth in direct testimony and cross-examination questions for the opposing expert. Any deficiencies in the evidence should be discussed with the attorney and introduced in trial during the direct testimony. If a questioned signature is a photocopy rather than an original document, include the research *An Evaluation of Line Quality in Photocopied Signatures* (Dawson and Lindblom, 1998), which found that line quality characteristics could be evaluated in average quality copies, and *Investigating Forensic Document Examiners' Skill Relating to Opinions on Photocopied Signatures* (Found and Rogers, 2005), which determined that FDEs could come to correct conclusions in photocopied signature cases.

Review Case File

Following the pretrial conference, the FDE must prepare herself in general for trial. Reread all correspondence in the case. Review notes, photocopies of evidence, test results, and the report. Read the latest legal opinions and current questioned document literature on the ABFDE and ASQDE websites. Study current literature relevant to FDE in the *Journal of the American Academy of Forensic Sciences* and the *Journal of the American Society of Questioned Document Examiners*. Read sections from questioned document textbooks that are relevant to the issues in your case.

Research the credentials of an opposing expert. Study any unfamiliar non-mainstream forensic science organizations listed on the opposing expert's curriculum vitae.

Organize the case file for court. Collect case correspondence and organize it chronologically. Group notes, photocopies of evidence, and charts in the case folder. Organize the case file with a 3-ring binder in large cases.

Make Court Chart

Lastly, make a court chart suitable for the court. Follow the agreement made with your attorney during the pretrial conference.

References

Dawson, G., Lindblom, B., 1998. An evaluation of line quality in photocopied signatures. Sci. Justice 38, 189–194.

Found, B., Rogers, D.K., 2005. Investigating forensic document examiners' skill relating to opinions on photocopied signatures. Sci. Justice 45 (4), 199–206.

Hansen, M., 2000. Expertise to go, ABA J., 44–52.

Riordan, W.M., Gustafson, J.A., Fitzgerald, M.P., Lewis, J.A., 2013. "Forensic document examination." In: Ubelaker, D.H. (Ed.), Forensic Science: Current Issues, Future Directions. Wiley-Blackwell, Chichester, West Sussex, UK, pp. 224–251.

Court Charts

Chapter Outline

Forensic Document Examination. http://dx.doi.org/10.1016/B978-0-12-416693-6.00011-4

Scientists, like game players, prefer to devise their own strategies, even though these depend on an assimilated, shared body of knowledge.

(S.E. Luria, A Slot Machine, A Broken Test Tube: An Autobiography, 1984)

Court charts directly demonstrate the science of forensic document examination. Each FDE prepares a chart in his or her own way. Charts generally consist of enlargements of questioned evidence juxtaposed with known materials in the case. They illustrate the opinion of the FDE.

Wet photographic charts, used in the last century, evolved into those produced with computers, scanners, digital imaging software, and printers (Hicks et al., 2006). One type of chart uses digital slides created with presentation software. The slides are projected with a computer projector. The enlargement feature on a photocopier generates paper enlargements of evidence for another kind of simple chart.

Before making a court chart, consider what type of presentation the case requires (ibid). Options abound for the FDE. Some possibilities include:

1. Enlargements of evidence mounted on foam board.

2. Handheld enlarged personal paper charts.

3. Slides created with presentation software and projected.

4. Video.

5. ELMO (a projector for opaque items) projected letter-sized paper charts.

Consider how many charts need to be constructed. Several charts that demonstrate a few specific features prove more effective than one chart containing many features (ibid). In a handwriting example, attention is focused better with one questioned signature and four known signatures than with two questioned signatures and 10 known signatures on one chart. Arranging one enlarged questioned signature and one enlarged known signature effectively focuses attention on specific features on the chart. More charts expressing fewer ideas on each one helps the judge and jury keep their focus narrowly targeted (ibid).

When using computer-projected presentations in court, a backup plan provides safety in case of technical difficulties with equipment. Bring paper copies of the computer presentation slides as a backup plan. Also pack an extra thumb drive containing the evidence presentation in case the computer in which the presentation is loaded has technical difficulties in court.

Discuss with your attorney what evidence in the case will be introduced at trial. Only use items on your charts that will be introduced in court. If you include evidence on your chart that you worked in the case, but the attorney decides not to introduce it into evidence at trial, the charts will not be admitted (ibid). The charts should be relevant to the case and representative of the evidence. Effective handwriting charts arrange the questioned writing above the known writings contemporaneous with the questioned writing. Known writings on the chart should be as close as possible to the date of the questioned writing.

Demonstration of evidence like different inks shown with infrared luminescence, typewriter character differences, and latent indented material recovered with an Electrostatic Detection Device (EDD) may require specialized charts and explanations in court (Ellen, 2006). Photomicrographs magnify small parts of a disputed document (ibid). These should be related to the overall view of the evidence item from which the photomicrograph was derived. Photomicrographs may be taken with a digital camera mounted on a microscope or with a handheld digital microscope like the MiScope. Unnatural pen lifts and tremor found in simulated signatures can be demonstrated with photomicrographs.

Computer-capture devices useful in digital chart preparation include:

1. Flatbed scanner

2. Digital camera

3. MiScope digital microscope

4. Video Spectral Comparator (VSC)

Once images of the evidence are captured, the images may require editing. Image editing software allows images of evidence to be cropped, rotated, brightened, enlarged, or reduced, along with many other options (Hicks et al., 2006). Image editing should be performed on a copy of the original evidence. The original captured images should be saved in a separate file and preserved. The original images are then available to show their condition prior to image editing used to clarify the images for a chart. Most charts use grayscale settings unless color is necessary for the evidence demonstration.

Photoshop Chart

Four current methods used to create effective court charts were gathered from FDEs in private practice and one from a government laboratory. These charts reflect an array of styles and computer software programs available for chart preparation and presentation. The first type of chart was made with Adobe Photoshop CS2 and was presented by Katherine Schoenberger at the American Society of Questioned Document Examiners (ASQDE) Annual Meeting in 2013 (Schoenberger, 2013). Adobe Photoshop was used to make a chart to support the findings in a case, and then it was attached to the report. This chart could also be presented in court, but the illustrations presented in the chart may be persuasive enough to keep the case from going to court. All images were captured with a flatbed scanner at 300 ppi. Images were saved in a lossless file format like a TIFF. Questioned and known signatures were cut and pasted onto the chart. The move tool was used to arrange the position of each evidence item on the chart. Each item was then labeled with the text tool.

Arrows were made with the line tool, and numbers were added to label features on the chart. Printing out the chart on a color laser printer or inkjet printer on good quality paper finished the process. Figure 11.1 shows a sample chart made with Adobe Photoshop CS2.

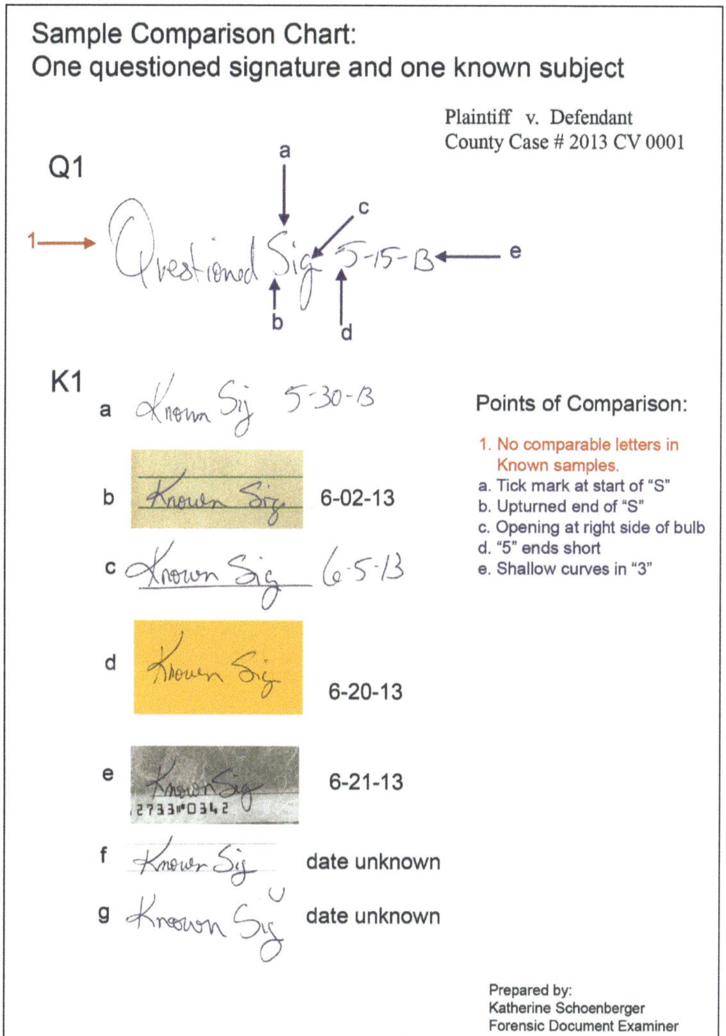

FIGURE 11.1 Chart created using Adobe Photoshop CS2 software. (*Used with permission from Katherine Schoenberger*)

PowerPoint Chart

A basic process for constructing a simple court chart in PowerPoint was presented at the American Society of Questioned Document Examiners (ASQDE) 2013 Annual Meeting by Dennis Ryan (Ryan, 2013). Signatures were scanned with a flatbed scanner and enlarged 2 to 4 times, depending on the original size of the writing. The images were copied into a blank PowerPoint slide. Text boxes were used to label each image on the slide. Colored arrows were created along with numbers and a legend of descriptive features on the slide. The electronic PowerPoint file should be brought to court along with paper copies in case of technical problems with the computer or projector in court. The paper copies of the chart may be projected with an ELMO or passed out to the judge, attorneys, and jurors. This is a quick and easy method for court chart preparation. Figure 11.2 depicts a chart created using PowerPoint.

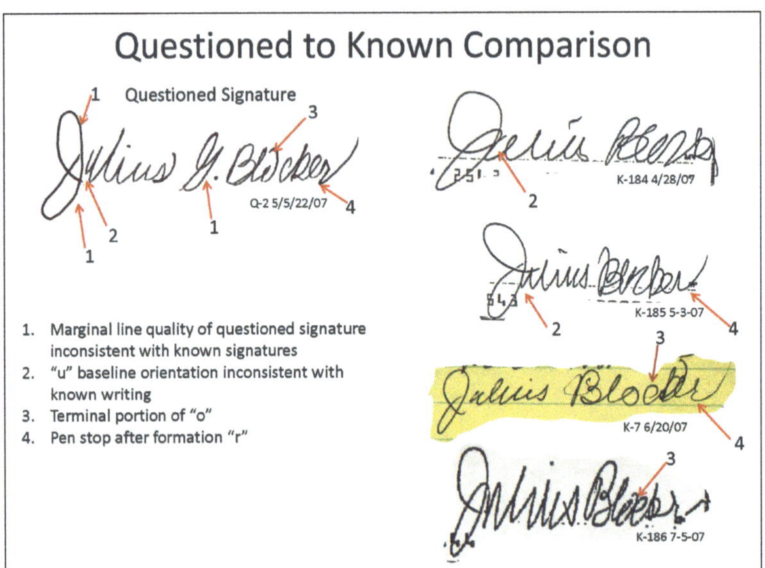

FIGURE 11.2 Chart created using PowerPoint software. *Used with permission from Dennis J. Ryan.*

Write-on 2 Chart

Brian Lindblom presented another method of chart preparation at the American Society of Questioned Document Examiners (ASQDE) Annual Meeting in 2013 (Lindblom, 2013). He used Write-On 2 Software to construct demonstrative charts. The following basic steps are included in Lindblom's method (ibid):

1. Choose a resolution of 300–600 ppi. Use 300 ppi for average-sized writing.

2. Consider the scale setting if the handwriting needs to be enlarged. If the enlargement is 2×, 600 ppi resolution will be required.

3. Assign Questioned and Known items Document Properties and select a Scale factor.

4. Generate Occurrence charts and select images to send to a report.

5. Select columns and rows for the images to be arranged in the report (reports are charts in this program).

6. Format the images listed.

7. View formatted report.

Images may also be exported to another software program for image editing. Figures 11.3 and 11.4 are charts created using images from Write-On 2 reports that were then exported to other software programs for further editing.

FIGURE 11.3 This case was worked using Write-On 2 software. The images from the Write-On 2 report were exported to Adobe Photoshop for cropping. The images were then brought into Adobe Freehand and formatted. *Used with permission from Brian Lindblom.*

PowerPoint with Hyperlinks

Brett Bishop presented an additional method of chart construction at the American Society of Questioned Document Examiners (ASQDE) Annual Meeting in 2013 (Bishop, 2013). Hyperlinks in PowerPoint were used to allow slides to be presented out of order

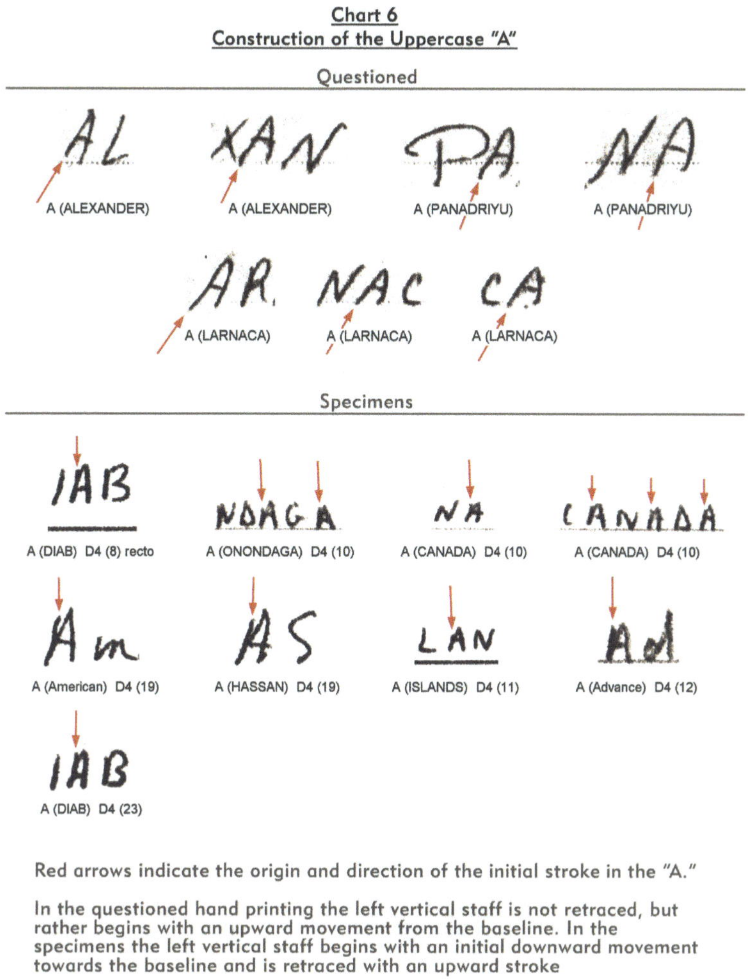

FIGURE 11.4 The comparisons in this case were done using Write-On 2 software. The character images were captured in the Write-On 2 report and exported to Adobe Photoshop for cropping and layout. *Used with permission from Brian Lindblom.*

rather than simply in sequence. During the PowerPoint slide show it is possible to jump to a slide that was selected with a hyperlink and then hyperlink back to the home menu slide. The feature also allows a hyperlink to a different presentation or to a custom supporting show. Figures 11.5–11.7 show examples of PowerPoint slides of charts attached with hyperlinks.

FIGURE 11.5 Chart created using PowerPoint slides with hyperlinks showing a questioned note with boxes highlighting letters to be hyperlinked to known letters for comparison. *Used with permission from Brett Bishop.*

FIGURE 11.6 Chart created using PowerPoint slides with hyperlinks showing questioned "NO" above and "N" in "DEFENDANT" below from known writing sample for comparison. *Used with permission from Brett Bishop.*

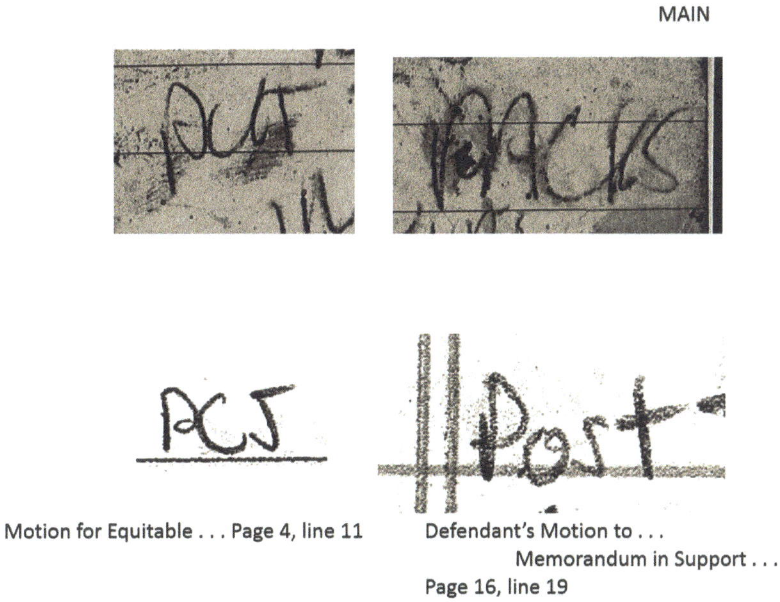

FIGURE 11.7 Chart created using PowerPoint slides with hyperlinks showing "PUT" and "PACKS" from the questioned note above compared to known writings "PCJ" and "POST" below. *Used with permission from Brett Bishop.*

Conclusion

Court charts can be created in many effective and diverse ways. Digital and electronic methods are the simplest and most common. The trend is to demonstrate a few significant characteristics on each chart. Today more charts are generated with fewer ideas per chart. The most effective chart presentations use a few targeted identifying details on each chart. The type of chart depends on the technical facilities of the courtroom and the preference of the FDE, the attorney, and the judge in the case.

References

Bishop, B., August, 2013. Using Hyperlinks in Power Point. Presentation at the Annual Meeting of the American Society of Questioned Document Examiners in Indianapolis, Indiana.

Ellen, D., 2006. Scientific Examination of Documents: Methods and Techniques, Third ed. CRC Press, Taylor and Francis Group, Boca Raton, Florida.

Hicks, F., Lindblom, B., Gervais, R., 2006. "Demonstrative Charts." In: Kelly, J.S., Lindblom, B. (Eds.), Scientific Examination of Questioned Documents, Second ed. CRC Press, Taylor and Francis Group, Boca Raton, Florida, pp. 375–382.

Lindblom, B., August, 2013. A Step by Step Guide to the Preparation of Demonstrative Charts Using Write-On 2 Software. Presentation at the Annual Meeting of the American Society of Questioned Document Examiners, in Indianapolis, Indiana.

Ryan, D., August, 2013. Court Charts Made Easy. Presentation at the Annual Meeting of the American Society of Questioned Document Examiners in Indianapolis, Indiana.

Schoenberger, K., August, 2013. Chart Preparation Using Adobe Photoshop CS2. Presentation at the Annual Meeting of the American Society of Questioned Document Examiners in Indianapolis, Indiana.

CHAPTER 12

Questioned Document Research Present and Future

Chapter Outline

Forensic Document Examination. http://dx.doi.org/10.1016/B978-0-12-416693-6.00012-6

Everyone knows that in research there are no final answers, only insights that allow one to formulate new questions.

(S.E. Luria, A Slot Machine, A Broken Test Tube: An Autobiography, 1984)

Introduction

Research covers a broad range of topics in forensic document examination. This chapter organizes research according to a few particular subject areas. The NAS Report called for more research in forensic document examination. A listing of research from the last ten years provides a sampling of research in forensic document examination that supports the foundations of forensic document examination. The NIST conference in 2013 delivered an array of current research in forensic handwriting examination by bringing forensic document examiners and researchers from the private sector and universities together. Published research on digital signatures points toward the future in forensic document examination. Frequencies of handwriting characteristics in large populations continue to occupy the attention of forensic document examiners as a research topic. A list of relevant textbooks completes the chapter by providing a sense of history and the most up-to-date writing on the subject.

A robust culture of research developed in the forensic document examination community during the last ten years. Forensic document examiners (FDEs) present their research at international, national, and regional forensic science meetings sponsored by the following organizations: the International Association of Forensic Sciences (IAFS), the Canadian Society of Forensic Science (CSFS), the American Society of Questioned Document Examiners (ASQDE), the American Academy of Forensic Sciences (AAFS), the Midwestern Association of Forensic Scientists (MAFS), the Mid-Atlantic Association of Forensic Scientists (MAAFS), the Southwestern Association of Forensic Document Examiners (SWAFDE), and the Southeastern Association of Forensic Document Examiners (SAFDE).

Research pertaining to questioned documents appears in the following scientific journals. The *Journal of Forensic Sciences* is a peer-reviewed premier forensic science journal and a product of the American Academy of Forensic Sciences (AAFS). AAFS was founded in 1948 and consists of 11 sections from a broad range of forensic specialties, including the Questioned Document Section (www.aafs.org). *Science and Justice* is a journal of the Forensic Science Society. This international organization includes members from more than 60 countries, with the majority of members being scientists from the United Kingdom (www.scienceandjusticejournal.com). *The Journal of the American Society of Questioned Document Examiners* is a peer-reviewed publication of The American Society of Questioned Document Examiners (ASQDE), and is published twice yearly (since 1998). The journal features articles pertaining to forensic document examination. Members and non-members may submit articles (www.asqde.org). The *International Journal of Forensic Document Examiners* originated in Canada and has ceased publication. It presented peer-reviewed research on FDE topics. The *Canadian Society of Forensic Science Journal* is a product of the Canadian Society of Forensic Science. It publishes original research from various forensic science disciplines, including questioned documents (www.csfs.ca). *Forensic Science International* is an international journal published by Elsevier. It publishes original research from many forensic science specialties, including forensic document examination (www.fsijournal.org). The *Journal of Criminal Law and Criminology* is a publication of Northwestern University Law School. Since 1910, it has published articles by legal scholars and criminological research (http://scholarlycommons.law.northwestern.edu/jclc/). Abstracts of research presented in the Questioned Document Section of the American Academy of Forensic Sciences annual scientific sessions from 2002–2011 are available in *Forensic Questioned Documents Proceedings 2002–2011* (American Academy of Forensic Sciences, 2012).

NAS Report

In 2009, the National Academy of Sciences issued a report titled *Strengthening Forensic Science in the United States: A Path Forward,* commonly known as the NAS Report (Committee on Identifying the Needs of the Forensic Science Community, 2009). Certain recommendations were made in the report. One recommendation was the creation of a National Institute of Forensic Science. Chapter 5 of the report gave the committee's assessment of a few forensic science disciplines. Many forensic science disciplines were not reviewed. The committee had this evaluation of forensic handwriting comparisons (ibid):

> *The scientific basis for handwriting comparisons needs to be strengthened. Recent studies have increased our understanding of the individuality and consistency of handwriting and computer studies and suggest that there may be a scientific basis for handwriting comparison, at least in the absence of intentional obfuscation or forgery. Although there has been only limited research to quantify the reliability and replicability of the practices used by trained document examiners, the committee agrees that there may be some value in handwriting analysis.*
>
> *Analysis of inks and paper, being based on well-understood chemistry, presumably rests on a firmer scientific foundation. However, the committee did not receive input on these fairly specialized methods and cannot offer a definitive view regarding the soundness of these methods or of their execution in practice.*

It is difficult to assess how much importance forensic document examiners should attach to the NAS Report since the committee did not include one forensic document examiner. When lawyers engage me in questioned document cases, they expect me to educate them on all of the current texts and research in the field. It would not be solid case preparation for an attorney to prepare on his or her own in the specialized field of forensic document examination. FDEs know the current state of the science, relevant textbooks, and current literature. If the NAS committee were to study FDE research in the last ten years, they would find a significant amount of questioned document research from forensic science journals and in presentations to national and regional forensic science societies. Below is a sampling of questioned document research published from 2003–2013 in only two important forensic science journals, the *Journal of Forensic Sciences* and the *Journal of the American Society of Questioned Document Examiners*:

Aginsky, V., 2006. Using tlc and gc-ms to determine whether inks came from the same manufacturing batch. Journal of the American Society of Questioned Document Examiners 9 (1): 19–27.

Aginsky, V., 2012. Examination of paper and toner in page insertion/substitution cases using tlc, gc-ms and ft-ir microspectroscopy. Journal of the American Society of Questioned Document Examiners 15 (2): 3–15.

Akao, Y., Kobayashi, K., Seki, Y., 2005. Examination of spur marks found on inkjet-printed documents. Journal of Forensic Sciences 50 (4): 915–923.

Alkahtani, A., 2010. The ability of forensic handwriting examiners to judge the quality of signature simulations in an unfamiliar writing system. Journal of the American Society of Questioned Document Examiners 13 (2): 65–69.

Alkahtani, A., Platt, A., 2009. Relative difficulty of freehand simulation of four proportional elements in Arabic signatures. Journal of the American Society of Questioned Document Examiners 12 (2): 69–75.

Aloyoni, M., Gushaish, J., Zahrani, Y., 2010. Deciphering of counterfeit traveler's checks. Journal of the American Society of Questioned Document Examiners 13 (1): 1–7.

Annunziata Nicolaides, K., 2012. Using acceleration/deceleration plots in the forensic analysis of electronically captured signatures. Journal of the American Society of Questioned Document Examiners 15 (2): 29–43.

Balko, L., Allison, J., 2003. The direct detection and identification of staining dyes from security inks in the presence of other colorants, on currency and fabrics, by laser desorption mass spectrometry. Journal of Forensic Sciences 48 (5): 1172–1178.

Berger, C., de Koeijer, J., Glas, W., Madhuizen, H., 2005. Linking inkjet printing to a common digital source document. Journal of the American Society of Questioned Document Examiners 8 (2): 91–99.

Berger-Karin, C., Hendriks, U., Geyer-Lippmann, J., 2008. Comparison of natural and artificial aging of ballpoint inks. Journal of Forensic Sciences 53 (4): 989–992.

Bird, C., Found, B., Rogers, D., 2010. Forensic document examiners' skill in distinguishing between natural and disguised handwriting behaviors. Journal of Forensic Sciences 55 (5): 1291–1295.

Bishop, B., 2012. Frequency of selected hand printing characteristics occurring within a national population: the new international version bible across America. Journal of the American Society of Questioned Document Examiners 15 (2): 23–25.

Bojko, K., Roux, C., Reedy, B., 2008. An examination of the sequence of intersecting lines using attenuated total reflectance – Fourier transform infrared spectral imaging. Journal of Forensic Sciences 53 (6): 1458–1467.

Boshir, R., Platt, A., 2012. The use of simple dimensional measurements in the analysis of simulated signatures: a preliminary study. Journal of the American Society of Questioned Document Examiners 15 (2): 17–21.

Brazeau, L., Gaudreau, M., 2007. Ballpoint pen inks: the quantitative analysis of ink solvents on paper by solid-phase microextraction. Journal of Forensic Sciences 52 (1): 209–215.

Brown, S., Sin-David, L., 2007. Diary of an astronaut: examination of the remains of the late Israeli astronaut colonel Ilan Ramon's crew notebook recovered after the loss of NASA's space shuttle Columbia. Journal of Forensic Sciences 52 (3): 731–737.

Brown, S., Klein, A., Chaikovsky, A., 2003. Deciphering indented impressions on plastic. Journal of Forensic Sciences 48 (4): 869–873.

Budowle, B., Bottrell, M., Bunch, S., Fram, R., Harrison, D., Meagher, S., Oien, C., Peterson, P., Seiger, D., Smith, M., Smrz, M., Soltis, G., Stacey, R., 2009. A perspective on errors, bias, and interpretation in the forensic sciences and direction for continuing advancement. Journal of Forensic Sciences 54 (4): 798–809.

Bugler, J., Buchner, H., Dallmayer, A., 2005. Characterization of ballpoint pen inks by thermal desorption and gas chromatography-mass spectrometry. Journal of Forensic Sciences 50 (5): 1209–1214.

Bugler, J., Buchner, H., Dallmayer, A., 2008. Age determination of ballpoint pen ink by thermal desorption and gas chromatography - mass spectrometry. Journal of Forensic Sciences 53 (4): 982–988.

Caine, R., 2012. Book review of: The neuroscience of handwriting: applications for forensic document examination, by Caligiuri, M., and Mohammed, L. Journal of the American Society of Questioned Document Examiners 15 (2): 27.

Causin, V., Casamassima, R., Marega, C., Maida, P., Schiavone, S., Marigo, A., Villari, A., 2008. The discrimination potential of ultraviolet–visible spectrophotometry, thin layer chromatography, and Fourier transform infrared spectroscopy for the forensic analysis of black and blue ballpoint inks. Journal of Forensic Sciences 53 (6): 1468–1473.

Chaikovsky, A., Brown, S., Sin David, L., Balmon, M., Barzovski, M., 2003. Color separation of signature and stamp inks to facilitate handwriting examination. Journal of Forensic Sciences 48 (6): 1396–1405.

Cheng, N., Lee, G., Yap, B., Lee, L., Tan, S., Tan, K., 2005. Investigation of class characteristics in English handwriting of three main racial groups: Chinese, Malay, and Indian in Singapore. Journal of Forensic Sciences 50 (1): 177–184.

Chim, J., Li, C., Poon, N., Leung, S., 2004. Examination of counterfeit banknotes printed by all-in-one color inkjet printers. Journal of the American Society of Questioned Document Examiners 7 (2): 69–76.

De Koeijer, J., Berger, C., Glas, W., Madhuizen, H., 2006. Gelatine lifting, a novel technique for the examination of indented writing. Journal of Forensic Sciences 51 (4): 908–914.

Dunn, J., Siegel, J., Allison, J., 2003. Photodegradation and laser desorption mass spectrometry for the characterization of dyes used in red pen inks. Journal of Forensic Sciences 48 (3): 652–657.

Durina, M., Caligiuri, M., 2009. The determination of authorship from a homogenous group of writers. Journal of the American Society of Questioned Document Examiners 12 (2): 77–90.

Dyer, A., Found, B., Rogers, D., 2006. Visual attention and expertise for forensic signature analysis. Journal of Forensic Sciences 51 (6): 1397–1404.

Dyer, A., Found, B., Rogers, D., 2008. An insight into forensic document examiner expertise for discriminating between forged and disguised signatures. Journal of Forensic Sciences 53 (5): 1154–1159.

Elliott, H., Stadmeyer, L., 2012. Stone paper: an overview of its characteristics and the impact they may have on forensic document examinations. Journal of the American Society of Questioned Document Examiners 15 (1): 11–29.

Ezcurra, M., Velasco, I., Gongora, M., Maguregui, M. I., Alonso, R., 2009. Analysis of bic crystal medium ballpoint pen inks. Journal of the American Society of Questioned Document Examiners 12 (2): 57–68.

Flynn, W., 2012. Conducting a forensic examination of electronically captured signatures. Journal of the American Society of Questioned Document Examiners 15 (1): 3–10.

Giles, A. B., Giles, A., 2009. Electrostatic detection apparatus enhancement using astronomical image stacking and processing software. Journal of the American Society of Questioned Document Examiners 12 (1): 19–25.

Green, J., 2012. Reliability of paper brightness in authenticating documents. Journal of Forensic Sciences 57 (4): 1003–1007.

Haddad, A., White, P., Cole, M., 2009. Examination of a collection of Arabic signatures. Journal of the American Society of Questioned Document Examiners 12 (1): 35–53.

Hammond, D., 2007. Validation of lab color mode as a nondestructive method to differentiate black ballpoint pen inks. Journal of Forensic Sciences 52 (4): 967–973.

Hicks, A.F., 2003. The handwriting testimony in the trial of Bruno Richard Hauptmann. Journal of the American Society of Questioned Document Examiners 6 (2): 97–111.

Hofer, R., 2004. Dating of ballpoint pen ink. Journal of Forensic Sciences 49 (6): 1353–1357.

Houlgrave, S., LaPorte, G., Stephens, J., Wilson, J., 2013. The classification of inkjet inks using AccuTOF DART (direct analysis in real time) mass spectrometry – a preliminary study. Journal of Forensic Sciences 58 (3): 813–821.

Iqbal, A., Majcherczyk, P., Weyermann, C., 2012. Statistical evaluation of the reproducibility and the influence of paper on the analysis of black gel pen ink using laser desorption ionization mass spectrometry. Journal of the American Society of Questioned Document Examiners 15 (1): 31–40.

Jasuja, O.P., Singla, A.K., Mand, M.K., Lyter, A., 2005. Examination of gel pen inks using physical and thin layer chromatographic examination. Journal of the American Society of Questioned Document Examiners 8 (2): 83–87.

Kam, M., Lin, E., 2003. Writer identification using hand-printed and non-hand-printed questioned documents. Journal of Forensic Sciences 48 (6): 1391–1395.

Klein, M., Aalderink, B., Berger, C., Herlaar, K., de Koeijer, J., 2010. Quantitative hyperspectral imaging technique for measuring material degradation effects and analyzing tlc plate traces. Journal of the American Society of Questioned Document Examiners 13 (2): 71–81.

Kruger, D., 2010. The longpen – the world's first original remote signing device. Journal of Forensic Sciences 55 (3): 795–800.

Lanners, B., 2011. Liquid lead pencils revisited. Journal of the American Society of Questioned Document Examiners 13 (1): 51–56.

LaPorte, G., 2004. Modern approaches to the forensic analysis of inkjet printing-physical and chemical examinations. Journal of the American Society of Questioned Document Examiners 7 (1): 22–36

LaPorte, G., 2004. The use of an electrostatic detection device to identify individual and class characteristics on documents produced by printers and copiers – a preliminary study. Journal of Forensic Sciences 49 (3): 610–620.

LaPorte, G., Ramotowski, R., 2003. The effects of latent print processing on questioned documents produced by office machine systems utilizing inkjet technology and toner. Journal of Forensic Sciences 48 (3): 658–663.

LaPorte, G., Stephens, J., Beuchel, A., 2010. The examination of commercial printing defects to assess common origin, batch variation, and error rate. Journal of Forensic Sciences 55 (1): 136–140.

LaPorte, G., Wilson, J., Cantu, A., Mancke, A., Fortunato, S., 2003. The identification of 2-phenoxyethanol in ballpoint inks using gas chromatography/mass spectrometry – relevance to ink dating. Journal of Forensic Sciences 49 (1): 155–159.

LaPorte, G., Wilson, J., Mancke, A., Payne, J., Ramtowski, R., Fortunato, S., 2003. The forensic analysis of thermal transfer printing. Journal of Forensic Sciences 48 (5): 1163–1171.

LaPorte, G., Arredondo, M., McConnell, T., Stephens, J., Cantu, A., Shaffer, D., 2006. An evaluation of matching unknown writing inks with the United States International Ink Library. Journal of Forensic Sciences 51 (3): 689–692.

Lewis, J., 2003. Striation patterns in new and used ballpoint pens. Journal of the American Society of Questioned Document Examiners 6 (2): 67–71.

Lewis, J., 2005. Indentation examination enhancement. Journal of the American Society of Questioned Document Examiners 8 (2): 65–69.

Li, C., Poon, N., Fung, W., Yang, C., 2005. Individuality of handwritten Arabic numerals in local population. Journal of Forensic Sciences 50 (1): 185–191.

Li, C., Poon, N., Yang, C., Poon, N., Fung, W., 2007. Significance of sequence of strokes in Chinese handwriting examination. Journal of Forensic Sciences 52 (2): 467–472.

Licht, G., Murano, E., 2004. ESDA effects in light of current discussions. Journal of the American Society of Questioned Document Examiners 7 (1): 7–21.

Lines, S.R., 2011. Book review of: Witness to forgery: memoir of a forensic document examiner, by Donald Doud. Journal of the American Society of Questioned Document Examiners 14 (1): 37.

Lines, S.R., Caradine, R., 2005. A study of business letter features. Journal of Forensic Sciences 50 (4): 924–927.

Mahajan, M., Arya, S., 2007. Examination of writings concealed by black pressure sensitive adhesive tape. Journal of Forensic Sciences 52 (5): 1212–1213.

Marquis, R., Bozza, S., Schmittbuhl, M., Taroni, F., 2011. Handwriting evidence evaluation based on the shape of characters: application of multivariate likelihood ratios. Journal of Forensic Sciences 56 (S1): S238–S242.

Masson, J.F., 2012. Scanned images: how well do they depict the subtle features in handwriting? Journal of the American Society of Questioned Document Examiners 15 (1): 41–47.

Mazzella, W., Khanmy-Vital, A., 2003. A study to investigate the evidential value of blue gel pen inks. Journal of Forensic Sciences 48 (2): 419–424.

Mazzella, W., Mathieu, A., Buzzini, P., 2006. Micro-Raman spectroscopy of color inkjet printed documents. Journal of the American Society of Questioned Document Examiners 9 (1): 1–8.

McGaw, E., Szymanski, D., Waddell Smith, R., 2009. Characterization of undigested particulate material following microwave digestion of recycled document papers. Journal of Forensic Sciences 54 (5): 1171–1175.

McGaw, E., Szymanski, D., Waddell Smith, R., 2009. Determination of trace elemental concentrations in document papers for forensic comparison using inductively coupled plasma–mass spectrometry. Journal of Forensic Sciences 54 (5): 1163–1170.

Mohammed, L.A., Ostrum, R.B., 2010. Using Adobe Photomerge™ for demonstrative evidence. Journal of the American Society of Questioned Document Examiners 13 (1): 23–32.

Mohammed, L.A., Richards, G., 2006. Thinking outside the box. Journal of the American Society of Questioned Document Examiners 9 (2): 77–84.

Mohammed, L.A., Found, B., Caligiuri, M., Rogers, D., 2011. The dynamic character of disguise behavior for text-based, mixed, and stylized signatures. Journal of Forensic Sciences 56 (S1): S136–S141.

Morris, R., Richards, G., 2010. What is the basis for a handwriting elimination? Journal of the American Society of Questioned Document Examiners 13 (2): 43–49.

Neumann, C., Margot, P., 2010. Considerations on the ASTM standards 1789-04 and 1422-05 on the forensic examination of ink. Journal of Forensic Sciences 55 (5): 1304–1310.

Ngan, S., McCormack, G., Novotny, M., 2005. The uniqueness of facsimile documents caused by changes in character pixilation. Journal of the American Society of Questioned Document Examiners 8 (1): 17–26.

Ning, L., 2011. A study of the stability and the utility of satellite droplets for classification of ink jet printers. Journal of the American Society of Questioned Document Examiners 14 (2): 35–45.

Nobles, K., 2010. An update of the typestyle classification program (type) into a Windows based format (wintype). Journal of the American Society of Questioned Document Examiners 13 (2): 37–42.

Olson, L., 2009. Indentations produced by the document feeder mechanisms of two black and white photocopiers. Journal of the American Society of Questioned Document Examiners 12 (1): 1–18.

Ostrum, R.B., 2006. Application of hyperspectral imaging to forensic document examination problems. Journal of the American Society of Questioned Document Examiners 9 (2): 85–93.

Ostrum, R.B., Tanaka, T., 2006. Another look at handwriting movement. Journal of the American Society of Questioned Document Examiners 9 (2): 57–69.

Parrett, D., Szabo, G., 2003. Lineup: the reliability of examinations involving multiple writers. Journal of the American Society of Questioned Document Examiners 6 (2): 82–84.

Radley, R., Lindblom, B., 2011. Impressions/ink intersection sequencing – a comprehensive overview. Journal of the American Society of Questioned Document Examiners 14 (2): 3–13.

Saunders, C., Davis, L., Buscaglia, J., 2011. Using automated comparisons to quantify handwriting individuality. Journal of Forensic Sciences 56 (3): 683–689.

Savoie, K., 2011. The frequency of occurrence of specific handwriting characteristics within a limited population. Journal of the American Society of Questioned Document Examiners 14 (2): 15–27.

Schuetzner, E., 2006. A study of attempted simulated signatures by teenage writers. Journal of the American Society of Questioned Document Examiners 9 (2): 95–103.

Senior, S., Hamed, E., Masoud, M., Shehata, E., 2012. Characterization and dating of blue ballpoint pen inks using principal component analysis of UV–vis absorption spectra, IR spectroscopy, and HPTLC. Journal of Forensic Sciences 57 (4): 1087–1093.

Simmons, D., Spencer, R., Auer, S., 2011. The effects of constraining signatures. Journal of the American Society of Questioned Document Examiners 14 (1): 39–50.

Srihari, S., Huang, C., Srinivasan, H., 2008. On the discriminability of the handwriting of twins. Journal of Forensic Sciences 53 (2): 430–446.

Sugawara, S., 2004. Comparison of near infrared light photography and middle infrared light photography for deciphering obliterated writings. Journal of Forensic Sciences 49 (6): 1349–1352.

Sugawara, S., 2007. Passport examination by polarized infrared spectra. Journal of Forensic Sciences 52 (4): 974–977.

Turnbull, S., Jones, A., Allen, M., 2010. Identification of the class characteristics in the handwriting of Polish people writing English. Journal of Forensic Sciences 55 (5): 1296–1303.

Vastrick, T., 2004. Admissibility issues in forensic document examination. Journal of the American Society of Questioned Document Examiners 7 (1): 37–47.

Welch, T., Bacon, C., Bacon, M., Bohn, S., 2010. Fracture match: a validation study of paper tears, part 1. Journal of the American Society of Questioned Document Examiners 13 (1): 15–21.

Weyermann, C., Marquis, R., Mazzella, W., Spengler, B., 2007. Differentiation of blue ballpoint pen inks by laser desorption ionization mass spectrometry and high-performance thin-layer chromatography. Journal of Forensic Sciences 52 (1): 216–220.

Wilson, J., LaPorte, G., Cantu, A., 2004. Differentiation of black gel inks using optical and chemical techniques. Journal of Forensic Sciences 49 (2): 364–370.

The NAS Report committee could also have considered the ten pages of questioned document research listed in the fine textbook *Scientific Evidence in Civil and Criminal Cases* by Andre Moenssens, Carol Henderson, and Sharon Portwood (Moenssens et al., 2007) for current texts and published papers. Interestingly enough, the NAS Repot committee chose not to comment on the non-handwriting aspects of FDE because they did not research the area. According to Budowle et al. (2009): *"Forensic science is evaluating itself and is improving its practices on a continuous basis. Improvement does not mean that the current practices are inadequate."*

The foundational research supporting forensic document examination appears in the following current questioned document and forensic science textbooks:

Scientific Examination of Questioned Documents, Second Edition (Kelly and Lindblom, 2006)

Scientific Examination of Documents: Methods and Techniques, Third Edition (Ellen, 2006)

The Neuroscience of Handwriting Applications for Forensic Document Examination (Caligiuri and Mohammed, 2012)

Forensic Science: Current Issues, Future Directions (Ubelaker, 2013)

NIST Conference 2013

The National Institute of Standards and Technology (NIST) hosted a forensic document examination conference on June 4–5, 2013, in Gaithersburg, Maryland. *Measurement Science and Standards in Forensic Handwriting Analysis* was sponsored by NIST along with the American Academy of Forensic Sciences – Questioned Document Section, American Board of Forensic Document Examiners, American Society of Questioned Document Examiners, Federal Bureau of Investigation Laboratory, National Institute of Justice (NIJ), and Scientific Working Group for Forensic Document Examination (SWGDOC). Speakers at the conference included FDEs from federal, state, and local crime laboratories and examiners in private practice, along with those from international laboratories. Researchers, statisticians, and an attorney completed the speaker list. The tightly targeted theme focused attention on the handwriting identification portion of the work of forensic document examination. Research was presented in a section on the foundational science supporting handwriting examination. One of the topics in this section was motor control and motor equivalence on handwriting (Caligiuari, 2013) which considered handwriting as a flexible motor skill. Another related subject in this section was handwriting stroke kinematics (Mohammed, 2013) which measures handwriting dynamically with a digitizer tablet and specialized software. An additional research project related to the foundational science supporting handwriting measured attention and the weight of handwriting features in considering what FDEs look at during handwriting comparison through the use of eye-tracking computer data (Merlino, 2013).

The NIST conference also offered presentations on reproducibility and reliability studies related to forensic handwriting identification. The skill of FDEs in identifying questioned handwriting from a homogenous group of writers who all attended the same elementary school in Brooklyn, New York, and were taught to write by the same group of teachers, was measured by Durina and Caligiuri (Durina and Caligiuri, 2009). The research found that FDEs participating in the study as a group averaged a score of 98% (ibid). In response to a critic of forensic document examination who suggested that a lineup of more than one suspect in questioned to known writing examinations may produce a different result with FDEs than an examination with questioned documents and only one suspect, researchers assembled a lineup of 1,000 individual writers and gave FDEs one questioned document (Parrett and Szabo, 2003). The FDEs compared one questioned document to known writing samples from 1,000 different writers. Each FDE who participated in the study identified the questioned writing with the correct known writer (ibid). The results further validate the individuality of handwriting and the skill of FDEs.

Quantitative systems for handwriting comparisons comprised part of the NIST conference. The Forensic

Language-Independent Analysis System for Handwriting Identification (FLASH ID) is a software program used to identify individual writers (Walch and Gantz, 2013). Graphemes (parts of characters, complete characters, or combinations of characters) are classified by their topology and geometric features (ibid). Statistical analysis of the topology and geometric features allows an individual's writing to be differentiated from that of other writers (ibid). This program is not yet in general use by FDEs.

Professor Sargur Srihari developed the software CEDAR-FOX (Srihari et al., 2008) and the newer software iFOX. These software programs are used by researchers in forensic document examination. They are not yet in general use in the FDE community.

D-Scribe is another software program used to recognize similar handwriting samples presented at the NIST conference. D-Scribe was designed to assist FDEs in identifying handwriting from different individuals (Schulte-Austum, 2013). The technology digitally converts and assists in interpreting handwriting through automation (ibid).

The NIST conference explored statistics for handwriting examination through current research projects presented. The NIJ research grant titled *Frequency Occurrence in Handwriting and Hand Printing Characteristics* applies statistical research to handwriting features (Vastrick, 2013). The goal of the project is to generate a list of the frequency of occurrence of certain handwriting features in order to determine how rare the features are in the general population (ibid). Statistical research applied to the time period for development of individual characteristics in the handwriting of children was also presented (Hanson, 2013). Individual characteristics will be identified by FDEs and scanned for analysis using iFOX handwriting software (ibid). The iFOX data will then be analyzed to generate likelihood ratios, which will suggest how frequently the individual characteristics may occur (ibid). Results of the study will statistically support the statement that individual characteristics develop in each person's handwriting as students move beyond the Copy Book handwriting method that they were initially taught (ibid). Preliminary computer evaluation of the frequency of certain handwriting characteristics in the general population was presented in *Statistical Basis to Determine Probabilities of Occurrences of Handwriting Characteristics*, (Srihari and Singer, 2013). The goal of the research is to provide quantitative support for the conclusions of FDEs in handwriting cases (ibid).

Research applying Bayesian methodology using likelihood ratios to quantitatively measure handwriting evidence added to the statistical section of the NIST conference (Marquis et al., 2011). A simulated case of a threatening letter measured the shapes of certain letters and compared them to the same letters from the actual writer of the questioned text and two other writers. Two propositions were considered: the suspect wrote the questioned text, or the suspect is not the author of the text and an unknown person wrote the questioned writing. The same documents in the case were tested with 100 random draws of the features considered in the case. This way the variability of the letters was considered. The results supported the hypothesis that the person who wrote the questioned letter also wrote the known writings submitted. Negative results were obtained with the two writers who did not write the questioned letter. These results supported the hypothesis of non-writership (ibid).

Legal implications in *Presenting Quantitative Techniques and Conclusions in Court* were presented by Kenneth Melson at the NIST conference (Melson, 2013). The need to better articulate handwriting comparison results using quantitative methods was suggested.

Other measurement tools related to handwriting discussed at the NIST conference included: the statistical functions of Write-On 2 software which allows the measurement of natural variation in handwriting (Lindblom, 2013), the consideration of the accuracy of depictions of subtle features in handwriting from scanned images (Masson, 2013), and the differences between low- and high-resolution images of checks scanned in the banking system (Lewis, 2013).

Digital Signatures

Electronic signature capture pads record our signatures at the grocery store, with couriers delivering packages to our homes, and even for insurance policy documents. FDEs have examined printed versions of signatures generated from electronic signature capture pads, and now the actual digital files may be submitted for examination. Forensic document examination is moving in a direction to include the examination of digital signature files in casework.

Signature capture pads use a stylus to record x-y locations and timing information. Rate of capture is typically 100 Hz or quicker (Flynn, 2012). Raw signature files may be used to digitally reconstruct the electronic signature using an Excel Spreadsheet (ibid). If only secure data is available, special software may be applied for forensic examination of the signature data (ibid). Raw signature files provide additional information beyond that offered in the inked signature, including: the timing of each stroke, the timing of acceleration and deceleration of the hand as it makes the signature, and the precise stroke sequence of the signature (ibid). Acceleration/deceleration data prove a long-held principle of forensic document examination that simulated signatures have a slow, drawn appearance (ibid). In Flynn's research, raw data files show quantitatively that simulated signatures take longer to write than genuine signatures (ibid). Raw signature file data in electronic signature cases goes beyond the low-resolution electronic signatures printed on paper. Electronically captured signature files contain information about the sequence of strokes and the speed of execution of the signature (ibid).

Annunziata Nicolaides continued Flynn's research by focusing on acceleration and deceleration plots in the examination of electronically captured signatures (Annunziata Nicolaides, 2012). She considered four hypotheses in her research:

1. Acceleration/deceleration plots will be consistent for each writer.

2. Different writers will have different electronic signature plots.

3. Simulated, traced, and spurious signature plots will differ from those of genuine signatures.

4. Acceleration/deceleration plot comparisons will be a helpful tool for signature identification by forensic document examiners.

The research found that each hypothesis was true (ibid). Acceleration/deceleration plots should be considered in analysis along with dynamic information and graphs of plotted signatures (ibid).

Future Forensic Document Examination Research

Researchers continue to examine the frequency of occurrence of handwriting and hand printing characteristics with large population studies in order to assess the rarity of certain features. The hand printing of 31,000 writers provided a varied group of writers who participated in writing scripture verses in a hand printed Bible project (Bishop, 2012). Bishop assessed the frequency of certain hand printed characteristics from this pool of diverse writers (ibid).

More FDEs will work with statisticians to further strengthen the foundation of the science supporting FDE.

Image capture devices will produce better, higher resolution electronic images of documents in every-day business considered by FDEs.

Computer software and automated systems like the Forensic Information System for Handwriting (FISH), Forensic Language-Independent Analysis System for Handwriting Identification (FLASH ID), D-Scribe, CEDAR-FOX, and iFOX will continue to develop and expand into general use, further assisting FDEs in their work. Write-On 2 software is already in common use by FDEs.

More FDEs will seek certification from the American Board of Forensic Document Examiners (ABFDE).

The Scientific Working Group for Forensic Document Examination (SWGDOC) will continue the development of new standards for FDEs and update the 21 existing standards.

Research will continue with more funding for forensic document examination projects. The comparative methodology of forensic document examination will continue to be enhanced by basic research and new technologies to assist us in improving the science.

References

American Academy of Forensic Sciences, 2012. Forensic Questioned Documents Proceedings. 2002–2011, AAFS.

Annunziata Nicolaides, K., 2012. Using acceleration/deceleration plots in the forensic analysis of electronically captured signatures. J. Am. Soc. Questioned Document Exam. 15 (2), 29–43.

Bishop, B., 2012. Frequency of selected hand printing characteristics occurring within a national population: the new international version bible across America. J. Am. Soc. Questioned Document Exam. 15 (2), 23–25.

Budowle, B., Bottrell, M., Bunch, S., Fram, R., Harrison, D., Meagher, S., Oien, C., Peterson, P., Seiger, D., Smith, M., Smrz, M., Soltis, G., Stacey, R., 2009. A perspective on errors, bias, and interpretation in the forensic sciences and direction for continuing advancement. J. Forensic Sci. 54 (4), 798–809.

Caligiuri, M., June 4, 2013. Neuroscience behind Motor Control and Motor Equivalence of the Handwriting Function. Presentation at the Measurement Science and Standards in Forensic Handwriting Analysis Conference sponsored by NIST in Gaithersburg, Maryland.

Caligiuri and Mohammed, 2012. The Neuroscience of Handwriting Applications for Forensic Document Examination. CRC Press, Taylor & Francis Group, Boca Raton, Florida.

Committee on Identifying the Needs of the Forensic Science Community, National Research Council of The National Academies, 2009. Strengthening forensic science in the United States: a path forward. The National Academies Press, Washington, D.C., pp. i-xx plus p. 328.

Durina, M., Caligiuri, M., 2009. The Determination of Authorship from a Homogenous Group of Writers. J. Am. Soc. Questioned Document Exam. 12 (2), 77–90.

Ellen, D., 2006. Scientific Examination of Documents Methods and Techniques, Third ed. CRC Press, Taylor & Francis Group, Boca Raton, Florida.

Flynn, W., 2012. Conducting a forensic examination of electronically captured signatures. J. Am. Soc. Questioned Document Exam. 15 (1), 3–10.

Hanson, L., June 5, 2013. Understanding Individuality of Handwriting Using Score-Based Likelihood Ratios. Presentation at the Measurement Science and Standards in Forensic Handwriting Analysis Conference sponsored by NIST in Gaithersburg, Maryland.

Kelly, J.S., Lindblom, B., 2006. Scientific Examination of Questioned Documents, Second Edition. CRC Press, Taylor & Francis Group, Boca Raton, Florida.

Lewis, J., June 5, 2013. Bank Check Scanning Practices. Presentation at the Measurement Science and Standards in Forensic Handwriting Analysis Conference sponsored by NIST in Gaithersburg, Maryland.

Lindblom, B., June 5, 2013. Using the Statistical Functions of Write-On 2 Software to Assess Natural Variation in Handwriting. Presentation at the Measurement Science and Standards in Forensic Handwriting Analysis Conference sponsored by NIST in Gaithersburg, Maryland.

Marquis, R., Bozza, S., Schmittbuhl, M., Taroni, F., 2011. Handwriting evidence evaluation based on the shape of characters: application of multivariate likelihood ratios. J. Forensic Sci. 56 (S1), S238–S242.

Masson, J.F., 2013. Scanned images: how well do they depict the subtle features in handwriting? J. Am. Soc. Questioned Document Exam. 15 (1), 41–47.

Melson, K., June 5, 2013. Presenting Quantitative Techniques and Conclusions in Court. Presentation at the Measurement Science and Standards in Forensic Handwriting Analysis Conference sponsored by NIST in Gaithersburg, Maryland.

Merlino, M., June 4, 2013. Cognitive Theoretical Perspectives in Studies of Forensic Document Examination including "What Examiners Look At" (i.e. Eye-tracking). Presentation at the Measurement Science and Standards in Forensic Handwriting Analysis Conference sponsored by NIST in Gaithersburg, Maryland.

Moenssens, A., Henderson, C., Portwood, S., 2007. Scientific Evidence in Civil and Criminal Cases. Foundation Press, Thomson West.

Mohammed, L., June 4, 2013. Handwriting Stroke Kinematics. Presentation at the Measurement Science and Standards in Forensic Handwriting Analysis Conference sponsored by NIST in Gaithersburg, Maryland.

Parrett, D., Szabo, G., 2003. Lineup: the reliability of examinations involving multiple writers. J. Am. Soc. Questioned Document Exam. 6 (2), 82–84.

Schulte-Austum, M., 2013. Presentation at Measurement Science and Standards in Forensic Handwriting Analysis Conference sponsored by NIST. D-Scribe, Gaithersburg, MD, USA, June 4, 2013.

Srihari, S., Singer, K., June 5, 2013. Statistical Basis to Determine Probabilities of Occurrence of Handwriting Characteristics. Presentation at Measurement Science and Standards in Forensic Handwriting Analysis Conference sponsored by NIST in Gaithersburg, Maryland.

Srihari, S., Huang, C., Srinivasan, H., 2008. On the discriminability of the handwriting of twins. Journal of Forensic Sciences 53 (2), 430–446.

Ubelaker, D.H. (Ed.), 2013. Forensic Science: Current Issues, Future Directions. Wiley-Blackwell, Chichester, West Sussex, UK.

Vastrick, T., June 5, 2013. Trends in Frequency Occurrence of Handwriting and Hand Printing Characteristics. Presentation at the Measurement Science and Standards in Forensic Handwriting Analysis Conference sponsored by NIST in Gaithersburg, Maryland.

Walch, M., Gantz, D., June 4, 2013. The Forensic Language-Independent Analysis System for Handwriting Identification (FLASH ID). Presentation at the Measurement Science and Standards in Forensic Handwriting Analysis Conference sponsored by NIST in Gaithersburg, Maryland.

Additional Reading

1. *Questioned Documents*, Albert S. Osborn, 1929 edition.
2. *Ames on Forgery*, Daniel T. Ames, reprinting of the 1901 edition.
3. *The Problem of Proof*, Albert S. Osborn, reprinting of 1926 edition.
4. *Evidential Documents*, James V. P. Conway, 1959.
5. *Suspect Documents*, Wilson R. Harrison, reprinting of 1958 edition.
6. *The Scientific Examination of Questioned Documents*, Ordway Hilton, 1982.
7. *The Scientific Examination of Documents*, David Ellen, 1989.
8. *The Scientific Examination of Documents*, David Ellen, Second ed., 1997.
9. *Forensic Examination of Ink and Paper*, Richard L. Brunelle and Robert W. Reed, 1984.
10. *Handwriting Identification: Facts and Fundamentals*, Roy A. Huber and A.M. Headrick, 1999.
11. *Forensic Handwriting Identification*, Ron N. Morris, 2000.
12. *Questioned Documents: A Lawyer's Handbook*, Jay Levinson, 2000.

13. *Speaking As An Expert*, Stephen C. McKasson and Carol A. Richards, 1998.
14. *Forensic Examination of Rubber Stamps*, Jan Seaman Kelly, 2002.
15. *Document Examination On The Computer*, Gary Herbertson, 2002.
16. *Forensic Digital Imaging and Photography*, Herbert L. Blitzer and Jack Jocobia, 2002.
17. *Analysis Of Paper*, B.L. Browning, 1977.
18. *Century Of The Typewriter*, Wilfred A. Beeching, 1974.
19. *The Chemistry of Synthetic Dyes and Pigments*, H.A. Lubs, 1955.
20. *Inks: Their Composition and Manufacture*, C. Ainsworth Mitchell and T. C. Hepworth, 1904.
21. *Thin-Layer Chromatography*, Justus G. Kirchner, Edited by Edmond S. Perry, 1978.
22. *The Pencil*, Henry Petrowski, 1999.
23. *Forensic Examination of Rubber Stamps: A Practical Guide*, Jan Seaman Kelly, 2002.
24. *Scientific Examination of Questioned Documents, Second ed.*, Edited by Jan Seaman Kelly and Brian S. Lindblom, 2006.
25. *Scientific Examination of Documents Methods and Techniques, Third ed.*, David Ellen, 2006.
26. *The Neuroscience of Handwriting Applications for Forensic Document Examiners*, Michael P. Caligiuri and Linton A. Mohammed, 2012.
27. *Forensic Questioned Documents Proceedings 2002–2011*, American Academy of Forensic Sciences, 2012.
28. *Forensic Science: Current Issues, Future Directions*, Edited by Douglas H. Ubelaker, 2013.

Index

Note: Page numbers with "*f*" denote figures.

FSC
www.fsc.org
MIX
Papier | Fördert
gute Waldnutzung
FSC® C083411

Kolibri 360 GmbH
Ferdinand-Jühlke-Straße 7
99095 Erfurt, Deutschland
produktsicherheit@kolibri360.de